Three Scuffed Suitcases

Three Scuffed Suitcases

Biography from the diaries Of Mary Elizabeth "Bess"
Shellabarger Colorado World War I Nurse

ALICE S. STEPHENSON

Library of Congress Control Number: 2015905417
CreateSpace Independent Publishing Platform
North Charleston, South Carolina

Dedicated
to
the memory
of
Emma Shellabarger Selch
and
Dorothy Selch Jeglum,
two amazing western women
of this
pioneer family.

Acknowledgments

Three Scuffed Suitcases is written with gratitude to many people. Mary Elizabeth Shellabarger (always known as "Bess") diligently recorded her daily journey and filed away the diaries in three scuffed suitcases; Emma Shellabarger Selch, her niece, knew the importance of this journey and retained the diaries, carefully passing them on to her daughter Alice Elizabeth Selch Stephenson.

Thanks to John Stephenson, who encouraged me to take the time to collect the thoughts and supported the process; to Glenn Selch for his encouragement and genealogy information; to Dr. Jeanette L. Sasmor, and the late Carol Irwin for manuscript review and editing skills; and to Robert Gardner for his title suggestion.

Gratitude is expressed to friends, family, and peers who helped in the learning curve to convert words written long ago into a story of interest.

Contents

I
Introduction

*S*mall entries in pocket-size books read as mundane as a dry desert landscape, but with time and closer inspection, they come alive in a colorful woven tapestry. Words create pictures, thread upon thread woven together in a pattern, building row upon row into something tangible and visible. Many notes made over a lifetime may be tossed aside with indifference, but ones that stubbornly remain, yearning to be seen, are destined to be acquired and read by the next generation and the next.

The San Luis Valley of Colorado had few women in 1879, and the tiny daughter born to Adam and Abigail (Abbie) Shellabarger on October 16 of that year made an impressive addition. The first girl of the family of five children, born with cleft lip and palate, in a small log homestead far from medical facilities, might have faced difficulty from the very beginning. The odds of this wee imperfect infant making a measurable contribution to her world, aside from possibly growing up loved and adding to the well-being of her immediate family, were staggering. Yet, from her daily diaries of varied sizes, some of soft suede and others of hardcover, written over many of her active eighty-three years, we find a story of a strong western woman, ahead of her time in focus, motivation, education, and wisdom. The legacy of Mary Elizabeth Shellabarger (known always as "Bess") is one of generous caring.

A lifetime of words and memories remained safely tucked away in three scuffed suitcases of varied vintage. This collection of diaries made a final move to Cornville, Arizona, after being shuffled from warm Arizona and California apartments to cold Colorado ranch storage rooms and then to closets in hot Arizona retirement homes. Their final resting-place was a storage shelf where they nudged and pushed into awareness the need to be reread and woven into a format of importance.

Bess wrote her diaries through much of her adult life, some in detail with each day chronicled and others in spurts with brief incidents jotted down in her characteristic penmanship. These diaries, stored away in her San Luis Valley ranch home for years, were marked in her writing, "Alice Elizabeth Selch will write my memoirs."

Bess, godmother and mentor of Alice, was the much-needed guide for her grandniece to follow her footsteps into the professional nursing world. The birth of the family's sixth generation, Elizabeth, in 2008, prompted exploration into these words written long ago. The information contained in each diary seemed to be meant to continue to inspire and motivate members of this family. The message was to be aware of imperfections in life's journey and turn them into growth and strength. The woman who speaks from these pages states loudly:

FOLLOW YOUR DREAMS,
STRETCH YOUR ABILITIES IN SERVICE TO OTHERS,
And
IMPERFECTIONS IN A BEAUTIFUL FABRIC ARE
OFTEN WHAT MAKE IT A MASTERPIECE.

Stories, interviews, pictures, drawings, letters, and notes from some of the many diaries will begin to tell the story. The sample of the 1904 diary and a page of the extensive letter Bess wrote home from her round-the-world trip as a young woman begin to unfold her legacy.

Sample 1904 diary and diary pages

II
Follow Your Dreams

The Suitcases

The morning sunshine came into the sitting area, lending brightness that she so enjoyed. The previous apartment Bess lived in was just so dreary. Her possessions seemed to fit into this one better, and she felt as if she would be at home here. Destinations were closer for her to walk to, and she could take advantage of the amenities of the college nearby. Organizing had long been her forte, but looking around this room, one would never guess it was something she did best. Leaning back against the small recliner, putting up her aching feet, and looking around the small duplex, Bess thought, "411 Mill Avenue, Tempe, Arizona," hoping she could remember that change of address. Looking back, she estimated this to be her forty-first mailing address in her eighty years. Sitting felt better after a long day of trying to arrange the boxes that the grandson of her previous neighbor, Mrs. Hoover, had so kindly hauled from the apartment down the street. It amazed Bess that she had collected all of this clutter, yet there was not much that anyone else would call possessions. She liked the fact that the built-in bookshelves would lend themselves well to the boxes of books. Oh, how she loved her books! She was beginning to feel grateful the rent went up on Seventh Street, as this cozy spot felt safe and adaptable to her lifestyle now. As she glanced into the far corner, she saw three suitcases of varied sizes, placed together as if hugging each other for dear life. Putting her feet down, she eased her small frame from the cozy chair and made her way around the book boxes to the corner filled with cases.

Popping the clasp on the first one, she carefully lifted the lid to reveal meticulously arranged booklets of all sizes. Picking up the closest one, she read, *"Diary-1900."* Bess marveled that she had not opened these memoirs for years. Maybe she would look back through them as she pondered a place for them. On top was the group she had started working with for her Life Story class. She had thought she would get farther with that project. Picking up a packet of typed pages from beside the diaries, she saw it was the beginning writings on her childhood memories.

These outlined the years before those first diaries. Her papa did a good job influencing his children to keep a daily record. Sister Eloise had just mentioned in her last letter that she had found several of Papa's diaries of his banking years. She said she was continuing her journaling, too. Turning over the manuscript pages, Bess wrote on the back, "Alice Elizabeth will write my memoirs." If she did not complete the job, her grandniece would understand her career and desires. Alice had recently written that she loved to write. Maybe when she had moments away from her nursing studies, she would work on this. Replacing the papers, Bess closed the suitcase and prepared for bed.

As was her habit, from her bedside stand she picked up the small red volume labeled "1959" and wrote, "Moved into new apartment." This was her first night in a new dwelling place!

The next morning, arising early, she glanced at her diary entry of the night before. Picking up a yellow pad of paper next to her bed, she quickly jotted down a list of all the addresses she could recall that had been home to her. This list got her mind working for the morning. (See Appendix 3.)

Bess enjoyed her tea in the little kitchen near the sitting area and began again to put the apartment into livable order. Midmorning she worked her way across the room to the three odd-shaped suitcases. Carrying each one to the bedroom, she started sliding them under the dust ruffle on her bed. The bookshelves were filled with books from the boxes, and this collection of diaries just would not fit there. Life's collections just didn't seem to have convenient storage places.

The third case did not slide under the bed as easily as its two companions did, and the buckle on the belt caught on the bed. Bess pulled it out again and sat on her footstool. Undoing the belt and clasp, she opened this case. The booklets were dated from 1918 to 1958. The diaries prompting her to think that maybe she should pick up the pieces and start her story. Who knew if anyone would ever be interested? She felt she had led a self-focused life. Someone would probably say, "Oh, she should have married and had children," or "My, what a selfish old maid," but as she looked back, she felt her experiences fit her well.

She had done far more than she would have dreamed in those early years, and she thought her parents would look with favor upon her journey.

Forty years of life were packed in one tidy box. It had not all been so tidy, she reminded herself, but it had been an amazing journey. Bess figured it should all be put together with a title: "Eighty Years in an Imperfect World." Replacing the band around the luggage, she carefully pushed this last case into its hiding place beneath the bed.

Frequently she would return to the diaries, stored under her bed, to reminisce and think about times gone by. She made an effort to arrange the diaries, pictures, letters, and information in the stored cases in some order of time and sequence.

Childhood Memories

$\mathcal{B}$ess was looking through a packet of written information included in her cases of diaries. She had stretched her memory, those years before, to come up with her earliest memories. She had written the following:

> *Father probably hitched up the horses to spring wagon when Mother told him he must start in time to get the Midwife, Mrs. Winker, who lived north across from the Lampon family on Cotton Creek line, six miles distant. I weighed five pounds and must have been a very peevish child, antagonistic to Mother as a way of getting attention. My brothers learned at school that boys do not play with girls and my little sisters had a lovely time playing together, mud pies and dolls, but I was very lonely. Sister Emma said she wished I had a twin so I would not bother them so much.*

Bess knew the new frame house the family lived in was built in 1883, when she was four years old. She had vague memories of that home. Bess liked to think of what brought her parents to her beloved San Luis Valley. The family history tells that story. Bess's parents began early in their lives to follow their dreams.

Adam, Bess's father, was born December 16, 1846, in Clark County, Ohio. He had come to Colorado in 1869, through Cheyenne, Wyoming, by Union Pacific Railroad, accompanied by his sister, Mary, her husband, Oscar Lehow, and others of the Lehow family.

The story told in writings about the family, which are stored in the Saguache County Museum, lets us know more about those pioneering days.

They went by stage from Wyoming to Denver. The family first settled near where Littleton-Denver Water Company and later the Martin Marietta plant were located. A large cattle company hired Adam, six months after his arrival, to trail herds from Texas through New Mexico to the Colorado San Luis Valley. In 1870, Adam took one hundred cattle on shares and filed a homestead preemption of 320 acres east of Moffat, Colorado, on Rito Alto Creek. He continued to take part in roundups from Poncha Pass to Taos, New Mexico, before the coming of barbed-wire fences. Adam raised cattle and horses until 1893. On April 3, 1873, he married Abigail Anna Wales, whose family were neighbors. Of this union were born:

1. Charles Walter   born August 8, 1875, in Moffat, Colorado.
2. Ralph Wales   born March 4, 1877, in Moffat, Colorado.
3. Mary Elizabeth (Bess) born October 16, 1879, in Moffat, Colorado.
4. Emma Irene   born April 27, 1882, in Rito Alto, Saguache, Colorado.
5. Clara Ethel (Dolly)   born March 7, 1884, in Rito Alto, Saguache, Colorado.
6. Gertrude Eloise,   born January 15, 1891, in Rito Alto, Saguache, Colorado.

Their son, Charles Walter (Walt), was the first white child born on the east side of the San Luis Valley. Home for several years was a small log cabin along Rito Alto Creek. The two sons, Walter and Ralph, attended one-room schools a few months each year, and each were sent to Denver to stay with relatives to attend some high school and business training. A house was purchased at 1732 East 175th Avenue in Denver, when the daughters were of school age, and Abigail spent the winters there with them. Emma Irene died of diphtheria at that home on October 5, 1894. Adam showed great affection for his daughters and indulged them. It was vitally important to him that his girls be worldly, educated, cultured, and able to hold their own in any situation. He hoped his sons would follow his example. Ralph did so as a cowboy, forester, businessperson, and rancher. Walter, also a cowboy, was more a lover of the ladies, and rebel. Adam died October 18, 1915, of liver cancer. It was told that a long cortege of cars and wagons filed from the Moffat railroad depot to the Rito Alto Cemetery, where Masonic burial services were held.

The local newspaper stated, *"Adam Shellabarger, 68, pioneer banker and holder of valuable Denver real estate was for years known as the wealthiest horseman and cattleman in Southern Colorado."*

The ranch house, Sangre de Cristo range in background

ABIGAIL WALES SHELLABARGER

Abigail's story was told by conversations and correspondence from her son R. W. Shellabarger. Abigail, born February 15, 1854, in Truro Township, Knox County, Illinois, was sixteen years old in 1870 when she, her two younger sisters, and her parents came west. They came by train to Cheyenne from Altoona, Illinois. Sixty dollars apiece paid for berthed sleepers. They continued from Cheyenne to Denver on the first real passenger train to arrive in Denver. Colorado governor Gilpin greeted them the day after their arrival. It took them six weeks by wagon to arrive in the San Luis Valley, where uncles of Abigail had prepared a house for them. Rumors preceded the family, and bachelors in the San Luis Valley were thrilled that some girls were coming to the country. Three months after they had arrived in the valley, Abigail (Abby) went with her father to borrow a sack of flour from where Adam Shellabarger was working on the Baca Grant. Abby and Adam were introduced, and apparently there was an immediate attraction. Frequent visits back and forth between the ranches were noted, and Adam and Abigail were married three years later.

Abigail was shy, having spent her entire life at the arduous duties of a pioneer homemaker. She had little energy for or interest in social life other than with her family and a few neighbors. Their home was strictly divided between "men's work" (outside) and "women's work" (inside). The boys were born in a small log cabin built by Adam's father on the homestead east of Moffat, Colorado. For several years home was this small log cabin. A Saguache carpenter, George Farrington, built them a nice frame house in 1883, which later burned.

Kegs of butter, which Abigail churned and generously salted, were taken to Pueblo to be traded for flour, sugar, and other foodstuff. Wild game and wild berries were common in their diet. The family living consisted of coping with nature with very little contact or material imported from the outside world. Ralph wrote of his earliest memory seeing his mother place buckets under the leaks from the dirt roof of the cabin to protect the beds, table, and stove when there were heavy rains.

Abby Shellabarger told her children of trips by covered wagon, stage-coach, early narrow-gauge railroad, and some of the first automobiles, and finally, around 1935, of a trip by airplane she took from Houston, Texas, to Pueblo, Colorado. She died September 12, 1943, at eighty-nine years of age.

The Shellabarger family at the ranch in 1900.
Walter, Dolly, Eloise, Abby, Ralph, Bess, and Adam.

The story passed down through the family of the infancy of Bess included what was indeed her first miracle. At her birth, when it was discovered she had a moderately severe cleft lip and palate, her father, Adam, inquired in Denver as to the best plastic surgeon of the time. Being a man of action and adequate means at that point, he sent his infant and her mother to Denver so that Bess could have her lip and palate repaired. Amazingly, that initial repair was adequate for her lifetime.

Family and friends noted that she had a rather large, flat upper lip, and many of her photographs are a side view at her request, but she seemingly suffered little from that early imperfection.

She attended early school in the one-room school on Cotton Creek attended by her brothers. When Moffat became a town in 1890, the schoolhouse was built there. In 1894, her father built a home in Denver, where she and her sisters attended elementary school.

A letter written by her little sister Emma addresses the day-to-day living during these years. Bess was in Denver and Emma still at the ranch.

Rito Alto Colorado February 3, 1894

Dear Sister,

It is very cloudy this morning. It snowed a little in the night. I wrote to Miss Rambo about two weeks ago. But haven't heard from her yet. Rafe received a little letter from Walter a few days ago. Rafe has quite a sore throat. But the rest of us are very well. Dolly and I and Florence Davis went over to Mr. Greers last Sunday and staid all day.

Mr. & Mrs. Tobler, their baby, and Clara, and Mr. Neidthardt were there the same day to see Mrs. Voorhees and the girls.

It was awful cold all day and we did not get home till almost dark. But we had a good time. Eloise wrote another letter this morning. Mamma asked her if she had improved in writing and she said "YES". She said "I want Bessie to get it but then I don't want to send it until spring". A week ago today Mrs. Davis borrowed our cart to take some eggs to town.

Mama sent for three copies of a fashion paper (The Vogue) in New York last week. But it hasn't come yet. It was quite clear this afternoon the sun is shining. Papa and Rafe went down to the lower place to take some cattle. We are getting from 2–4 eggs a day, all pullet eggs. We got twenty-one of the hens that hatched last summer. I suppose you received Papas letter and the check he sent. Eloise is busy playing with her doll. She has named her doll that Walter gave her DAILY. We don't know where she got that name. I suppose she heard Papa talking about the daily News. Florence and Walter Davis were here this afternoon to get saw dust to pack eggs in. Eloise still talks about going to the Kindergarten. I guess I can send this to the P.O. tomorrow.

Well, I can't think of any more to say, so I will close with love to all.

From your loving sister, Emma

P.S. Feb. 4, 1894: Mamma said to tell you that she didn't have to bake any more since Dolly and I and especially Eloise can. Dolly baked bread yesterday,

Eloise helped me to bake some gingersnaps, and she made some little rolls and calls them rollers. Well, Papa is ready to go to town, so good-bye.

Your loving sister, Emma

The town of Moffat, where Bess grew up, was established when the narrow-gauge railroad line was built between Villa Grove and Alamosa, Colorado. At one time four railroads converged at Moffat from all four directions, making it the second-largest shipping yard in the state. By 1913, water rights were not resolved, and the town, which had expanded to 3,874 lots, found its boom ended. The town remained the center of activity for the ranchers in that corner of the San Luis Valley.

Many people feel they cannot remember activities before the age of two, but Bess could recall a number of early childhood memories. (From diary entries:)

- *I remember the place where I was born. A log cabin with three rooms that was provided with a leak proof roof before I was born.*

- *I remember losing my bonnet, which I prized, when Mother carried me as she walked in the wind near the Littleton ranch. Family was looking for Smokey Topaz in the dry Cherry Creek bed. I also remember father giving my first vaccination (anti-smallpox), when I was 2 years old, as I sat on a table at our log home on the lower place.*
- *The Children's Sunday school class at Rito Alto Church, seated in a half circle around the teacher who drove six miles with a balky horse with buggy.*
- *Playing with dolls: I do not remember if I ever had a rag doll, but the first I recall was "Janette" a china head doll with regulation black hair glazed over its head. The second doll I remember was "Gracie", a wood doll that was left in the sun. She had a navy blue satin dress made by Aunt Matte, with shoe buttons on the front of a navy blue skirt. Then I had a beautiful bisque doll.*
- *I had pets; "Frisk" the gray & white cat that devoured dry wheat. Best of all was my riding horse "Felix" that was gored by a bull and had to be killed while I was away in Denver at High School. I grieved much.*

At age eleven Bess wrote a letter to one of her sisters when she took a short trip across the San Luis Valley from the ranch:

Creede, Colorado, July 27, 1897

The package Mama sent came all right yesterday and I was very glad to get the veil. When we got on the train at Moffat that morning the car was full of the queerest people and all looked like immigrants, but we finally got seats together. There are lots of nice wheat fields in the 41 country. Alamosa is a pretty place, there are so many trees there, and the Rio Grande is pretty though the water is quite low there. Monte Vista is the prettiest place we saw. There are a great many Mexican settlements between here and Monte Vista.

Del Norte is pretty too and the observatory up on a high hill out of town is conspicuous for a long distance. Mr. Major met us at the depot and we were driven in a buggy to their house in upper Creede as the depot is down in Jimtown. Bachelor is still up the canyon farther but we haven't been there yet. The P.O. at Jimtown is Amethyst, but this is just Creede.

We went to a whist party Saturday night and to church Sunday morning and they got a wheel for me and Mr. Major took Gertie and me for a ride in the evening. We went quite a way down the road toward the Gap and the road is just like a floor and the grades are not half as bad as expected. The worst grade is from Jimtown up here only about a mile and even then, we didn't have to dismount in coming up. Gertie went riding again yesterday afternoon. Mrs. Major had a high five party here last night and I had a lovely time.

We all have an invitation to go to a ball tonight, given by the Knights of Pythias and I guess we will go and dance till eleven o'clock as we have to get up early tomorrow as Mr. Major is going to take us all up to one of the lakes of the river. Perhaps we will stay one night, but have given up camping several days.

The Holy Moses Saloon is across the street from the store. Majors live over the store.

Lovingly, Your sister, Bessie

Another letter was written to Eloise from 2147 California Street, Denver, Colorado, when Bess was age thirteen and in the sixth grade.

Dec. 7, 1897

My darling little sister

I want to see you so bad. You can talk just as good as anybody now can't you. The girls are awful good aren't they to take care of you so nice and write me letters about you. You live in quite a small family now don't you? Aunt Lizzie still has the little dog Dick he is always very glad to see me when I go out there and jumps around me tickled to death. Do you still play with the girls in their playhouse on warm days if there is any down there?

How is old grey getting along and old Joe? Have you seen any more skunks, and been as excited about it as you were when I was there? You tell Emma I am just aching to have a horseback ride. I haven't had one since I have been here. Tell Mamma you have got to see Bessie.

I have got to see you, but it won't be long till we do see one another but it seems an age. I do hope I can get there the day before xmas, but if I don't you be sure to hang your stockings up and have the girls tell you all about it. I am getting so sleepy I guess I will have to go to bed. Oh, how I wish I could sleep with you tonight instead of alone. I will close with love to all.

Your ever loving sister Bessie Shellabarger
P.S. The sleighs go dinglinging by quite often and the people look like they were having a good time. Mrs. Lehow's hired girl came in from the ranch last Sunday and is going to stay here this winter. I am going to speak a piece tomorrow at school. I am getting along all right in the sixth grade but I have to study pretty hard nights at home.

The girls at school wear felt sailor hats and commodore caps more than any other kind of headgear. I think the ribbon Mamma colored looks just as good as new and everybody else does too. I am wearing my plaid dress to school now. They call when we eat dinner lunch and supper dinner. I will tell you what we had for dinner tonight as I often wonder what you have. We had roast beef, sweet potatoes, parsnips, apple pie, cooked tomatoes, bread and butter and jelly and apples and oranges. I guess your dress is all finished now but I can't wait until a week from tomorrow when I go out there. You have no idea how much different it is to live in town. Mrs. Lehow made some cough syrup today and had me take some tonight, I haven't got over my cough yet, but it is better

Your ever loving sister, Bessie

An additional letter found with the diaries was to her mother, written from 1732 Seventeenth Avenue, Denver, soon before she graduated from high school at age eighteen.

Dec. 19, 1897

My Dear Mama,

The meat came this morning while we were at church, and Mr. Withers took it in as Cheethams were gone too, he said the man didn't say anything about the charges for bringing it up and I don't suppose now he will make a special trip for the money. The meat was frozen so I put it in the cool-house, and Dollie took the chicken over to Mrs. Cheetham.

It was awfully good of you to fix those chickens so nice and even stuff them and I hope we will get time to cook one of them anyhow before it dries too much. We will both have more than usual to do this week as Dollie has her recitation to learn and I will have a test in every study before Friday. We get out Thursday, as the boys "Prize Speaking" is on Friday.

Dollie wants me to go down town with her tomorrow to get a waist. I didn't go to either the Attic or Lycenum meetings. I gave my tickets to Cheethams and Smiths. The commissioned officers of the girls' cadets are going to have a ball at Mabel Stearns house but I am an uncommissioned officer and am not in it as usual.

Dollie has her violet voile finished and has commenced one of holly, she does quite well considering how poor she is at common sewing. The machine is much nicer than Aunt Lizzies, the wood-work is beautiful and it runs nicely too.

It snowed again today as usual and is quite cold. I have to almost sit up with the pipes to keep them from freezing. It snows often in the night and I don't get time to clean the front walk before school it wouldn't do much good as it usually snows till about noon. And Mr. C shoveled it off last time when he did his, and the time before it froze on so that I couldn't get it off so when we came home from church Mr. Parks was digging it off from his and our, and I told him to let it go because I could get it off when it would get a little softer. He said he ought to do some Christian act because he had not gone to church at all that day.

The corner man has an old white balky horse now. I suppose the other finally got so it couldn't move. All for now.

Your loving daughter Bessie

Bess, 1897.

Included in the packet of papers were several pages on yellow pad written by her niece, Emma Shellabarger Selch, in Emma's distinct penmanship. Emma apparently started reading diaries to put the whole story of the early years in a concise capsule. Bess recalled that Emma sent her these notes after being loaned some of the diaries to read. Elaboration of the learning years renewed many memories. It was amazing that Emma could make all of those years appear so clear-cut and concise.

Emma's writing filled in more facts about the story. She, like Bess, often took writing classes, and these must have been her notes from one of her lifelong-learning groups.

This document pretty much tells the story of the learning years in a nutshell:

Bess attended school in a one room building on her father's ranch for a few years. In 1889 she visited her aunt, Elizabeth Wales Shellabarger (Lizzie) in Littleton, Colorado at the ranch of Will Shellabarger where she was home schooled and finished third grade requirements. She was instructed by Lizzie while her aunt was also cooking for haying crews on a small wood stove. Soon a house was purchased in Denver by her father and mother and three Shellabarger daughters lived there during the school year. Bess attended elementary and high school from this home. The second daughter, Emma, died there of childhood diphtheria and it was a very traumatic time for the other sisters. Abby, their mother had joined the Women's Club in Denver and under the club's supervision, a clay modeling class displayed Bess' work in 1903. Bess continued her artwork, one project being bookmark designs showing their home ranch house with the Sangre de Cristo Range in the background. These she used in her own books throughout her lifetime.

Book mark designed by Bess

Denver home. 1732 East Seventeenth Avenue, Denver, Colorado.

Bess graduated from East Denver High School in Denver, Colorado in 1899. Both Bess and Dolly attended Emerson College of Oratory in Boston, Mass. in 1901 and 1902 taking special literary courses. Some lessons, at this time, were taken in voice at the New England Conservatory of Music. Full credits from these years were accepted by Columbia University in 1916 when Bess entered there for her B.S. Degree. When back at home, during a summer away from school, Bess apparently became romantically interested in Ralph Garretson, a young man in Salida, Colorado.

Ralph Wykes Garretson, with whom Bess had studied and established a social bond, became her very special man friend. Bess celebrated the fact that she had found a "soul mate" in someone who shared her interests in books, religion, art, discussion, and politics. They apparently traveled to Denver to special programs and speeches and enjoyed long talks and sharing of information.

This small amount of information is mentioned in the diaries about this relationship. Ralph would have been twenty-five and Bess twenty-four when she noted, *"Ralph Wykes Garretson died September 7, 1903 at D.& R.G. Hospital after operation for ruptured appendix. It was then I decided to be a nurse and entered Belleview in June of 1905. Ralph was buried in Haight Lot on Dr. Jackson's lot in Salida."* A note accompanying Ralph's pictures states, *"Ralph W. Garretson died of peritonitis. He was buried on 11 Sep 1903 age 25, and rests in Section H of Fairview Cem, Salida."*

Bess stayed at home on the ranch but found herself at loose ends and unable to recover well from her loss.

Thus ended her childhood!

Ralph Wykes Garretson

Ralph's burial place

III

Stretch Your Abilities in Service to Others

Adventure Begins

$\mathcal{A}$ close friend of Bess, Mabel Ball (daughter of Robert J. Swither, retired US Army major), had married an army officer and was going to the Philippine Islands for a term of service. She asked Bess to accompany her and her lieutenant husband Lou as her companion to help with their two small children. Mr. and Mrs. Garretson (Ralph's parents) also accompanied them on this adventure. A clipping found in the 1905 diary stated, *"Elizabeth has become renowned as a traveler, she having made a trip around the world, starting on December 1, 1903, and returning in June, 1904. Her route was from San Francisco to Honolulu, then across the Pacific to Manila [sic], through the Indian Ocean, the Red sea, Suez Canal, the Mediterranean, and across the Atlantic and this continent to her home. She was one month on the water going and fifty-eight days returning."*

Another article in the local newspaper (the *Saguache Crescent*), titled "Early History of Saguache" and published in November 1903, told of the trip, beginning, *"Miss Bessie Shellabarger of Crestone has been spending several days in Salida as the guest of Mr. and Mrs. Garretson. She met Mrs. Mabel Ball of Denver here and together they started for San Francisco from where they will go to the Philippine Islands to stay for a year and a half. Mrs. Ball's husband is a U.S. Army Officer stationed on the islands."*

This trip was a happy choice for Bess, who would get to meet new people on the ship and enjoy the social life at an overseas base with parties and horseback riding with young army officers. She always had a sketchbook at hand and made many interesting drawings and small watercolors of the sights on the islands.

When her time in the Philippines was complete, she asked a friend to accompany her as her companion.

They returned to the United States by the Suez Canal and Singapore, thus completing travel all the way around the world. They stopped at the world's fair in Saint Louis upon their return.

This trip was an amazing feat for a ranch girl from southern Colorado.

Bess and Purr before leaving on trip.

Bess and Ralph on horseback at the ranch.

The following snippets from her daily diaries and letters to home give us a picture of her travels, beginning as follows:

<u>November 15, 1903</u>: I left Moffat for Denver and met Mrs. Garretson, staying with her in Salida overnight. Received an 8 a.m. telegraph from Mabel that she missed her train and would come the next day. At 11:30 received another dispatch that baby, Dorothy, was sick. I arrived in Denver the next day and spent the day with my sister Eloise and night with Mabel and Mrs. S. We bought our $25.00 tickets for train trip to San Francisco. At 8:a.m. Saturday, we left for California. Met Mr. & Mrs. Garretson in Salida. Mabel & I fell down running for lunch at Minturn. We had 3 a.m. breakfast at Heber, Utah and ate dinner in the Diner in Nevada. The baby cried all night to be held. The first green trees greeted us at Colfax, California and we reached Sacramento after dark. Stayed in Oakland in the sleeper all night.

Tuesday: November 26, 1903. It was a foggy day on our arrival to San Francisco. We went down town to check on transit. Had Thanksgiving Dinner at the Cliff House and went to church and shopping in "Frisco".

Monday December 1st: Started on Transport 'Logan'. It was foggy, but cleared passing under the Golden Gate. The baby cried all night and we found the Doctor for her. Attended a band concert on board in the afternoon, staying on deck most of the day. We sailed 302 miles in 24 hours. Food is good.

Monday December 7th: High winds, boat rocking and still frigid. Walked deck with pretty trained nurse. Went to baggage compartment to unlock trunk. Had first hot salt water bath and change of clothes.

Tuesday: December 8th: In sight of land, Molokai, the Leper Island. Landed in Honolulu at noon.

The following lengthy letter was well preserved and folded in the trip diary, having been written in 1903 and mailed from Manila. It is an education to read her letters, as they help the reader feel as if the trip is being taken firsthand.

Wednesday December 9, 1903
Dearest Dolly,
  The day was lovely without rain. We were ready to leave the boat early and with Dorothy in her buggy, we strolled through the streets to see the queer people and the beautiful vegetation and went shopping. Honolulu has many nice large brick and stone buildings and stores that are as up-to-date as anywhere. Curio stores are everywhere and fine large clean drugstores kept by Americans but with Japs or natives as clerks. There are beautiful homes and beautiful

drives bordered by palm trees and great shrubs of variegated plants. The flamboya plant and poinsettia blooms in profusion in nearly every yard. The most picturesque sight is the Japanese family sitting on their porches, the women and children so refined and dainty compared with the coarse big women of the native family next door. The Mother-Hubbard dress of light cotton material seems the local costume of the islands. To make them seem more horrid for street wear they are all cut with the front short and a train in the back. It is a relief to see the pretty little Japanese women with their beautiful headdresses and graceful gowns but their sandal shoes are very funny and they have to walk in such a shuffling way.

The Japanese children are often carried in sort of Indian fashion tied on the mother's back with a long piece of cloth twice wrapped around its body, leaving the baby a chance to look forward over its Mother's shoulders. We came back to the boat to lunch, and then went up town later with a lady in a carriage. We drove around town, mailed some letters and bought some flower wreaths for our hats. The native men and women wear these around their necks and hats and there is a corner down town where the natives sit and make them from carnations, a kind of buttercup and a lily. The colors are gorgeous and are very pretty. Later they were brought to the boat by vendors and also long shell and bead chains. At three-o'clock, the Hawaiian Band came on board, played for us, and sang, too. Do you remember when they were in Denver? I think they are much improved. Then General McArthur and his wife came on board, they happen to be in Honolulu now. When the Star Spangled Banner was played the men all took off their hats and a good many people looked very serious who were leaving friends behind. Our boat started again at five O'clock then the boys who had been swimming around near the boat began to dive for coins and they followed us half a mile from the pier. They can swim so well and easily, it is perfectly wonderful. The last one as he turned to swim back to shore shouted to us "Be sure not to forget to come back." Then the sun went down and we went in to dinner. Yesterday we were invited by Col. And Mrs. Robinson to go with them in the army ambulance to take the Poli drive, it was beautiful and the view at the end, where we looked down over the cliff into the valley below was grand.

We did not have time to go to the Punch bowl crater, and that is what I wanted to see most of all. We visited the Government Palace and went into the throne room of the old souvenirs of the Islands. In the evening the Inaugural Ball was held for the new governor who took the place of one who had been made Judge. We were tired and did not go because we would have had to get some good dresses from our trunks but many of our passengers went and danced the whole evening and some of the officers went as they were in Kahikan uniforms, that was not showing much respect for the government I think.

<u>Thursday Dec. 10, 1903</u>. We are well on our way again and the sea is no less rough so that many are still sick.

<u>Friday, Dec. 11</u>, It is cool and pleasant today we are going north from Honolulu to Midway. It is too windy to have the baby out on deck so we manage to get much reading done now. Mabel & I are reading to each other the history of Hawaii.

<u>Sat. Dec. 12</u>. We are looking forward to being vaccinated today. The whole upper deck must go through the ordeal before landing.

The soldiers were vaccinated yesterday. 5 p.m.--The doctor came to our stateroom and vaccinated all of us, it seemed wicked to hurt the baby's sweet little arm that way, but she soon forgot about it and went to sleep. A white sea gull was caught on deck and will be kept for a pet by the deck hands.

<u>Sunday, Dec. 13</u>. The Chaplain had services in the saloon at 10:30 again. Mabel went today and I stayed with Dorothy We had a big

dinner tonight, the waiter saved the menu card for me, and I will send it with this that you may see what a variety we have. We are going very slow and sounding all the time to avoid running into rocks. It is a very dangerous place and many of the people are dreadfully frightened for fear we can't go through the night safely. Monday— our boat has stopped four miles off from Midway Island and we are waiting for two of the life boats to return that rowed ashore with the mail and provisions. There are nine people living on the island, one woman. They had nine sacks of mail, mostly magazines and Christmas presents, we suppose. What a welcome sight it must have been to those isolated people to sight the transport this morning when they have not seen anyone for eight months. It is a cable station, but this is the first time a transport has stopped. We saw the boats lowered and loaded to be sent to land. The sailors got into the boat then it was lowered by pulleys from beside the upper deck. It looked very dangerous when it struck the water and was tossed up against the side of our boat before they could unfasten the ropes and use oars. Then I don't understand how such little boats could live on the breakers we could see tossing near shore, but they did and merrily rode the waves. Most exciting of all is the fishing going on now, several very big fish were caught with hooks about twice as large as trout hooks baited with beef.

The children are wild over every one that is pulled out. We have seen several sharks and the Capt., Quarter-master, caught one and pulled it to the surface but it got away. It straightened out the hook—a big hook, too, fastened to a strong three ply rope. Several of the men had their hands burnt trying to pull it up. There is one that must be 10 feet long; this one was only about four feet. It was funny to see one of the girls grab at a sailor who was trying to help pull, he did seem to be going almost overboard.

In the p.m., the two boats returned bringing the first news for two weeks from the outside world. A cable from Chicago said it was 20 degrees below zero there, it seems impossible when her it is so warm. It was very interesting to see the boats hoisted into place, when getting the pulleys attached again; the boat would rock and toss so that the sailors were thrown from their seats. The sailors have a singsong call they use doing such work. No more sharks were caught, though finally, a big rope was resorted to as a line and a regular beef hook baited with a "hunk" of salt park was used. It was all wildly exciting when those monsters would nibble at the bait. There are some playful kittens here in the saloon where I am writing and they are playing so I can hardly write.

Wednesday, December 16th: We lost Tuesday by going over the International Date Line. It has been too wet and rainy to go on deck much today, but we are going fast again making good time. This is Papa's birthday so I shall dress up extra much for dinner tonight to celebrate the occasion. I doubt if he is thinking half so much about it as I am.

Thursday, Dec. 17th: The ship has rolled and pitched all day and all night after the storm of yesterday. Pedestrians on deck are nearly thrown overboard. Eating is not the easiest thing when the soup has a tendency to spill all over the table.

Mabel and the baby are nearly sick from their vaccination but my arm is not getting sore.

Friday, Dec. 18th: Preparations for Christmas must make something doing for you at home now and we are doing nothing of the kind now, in fact, it does not seem that season at all. We had a good band concert this afternoon, and I had a long talk with the Colonel's wife and walked deck with the army nurse again tonight. The weather gets warmer and I become sleepier in fact I can't sleep enough.

Sat. Dec. 19th. The warmest day yet—but the sea is smooth at last. The soldiers gave a vaudeville show tonight—people sat on the stairs and leaned over the rail to see and the soldiers climbed up the masts and everywhere, songs, violin solos, clog dances and boxing matches. The violin solo was fine by one of the signal corpsmen who used to play in the Boston Symphony. I should like to have had a flash light picture of the audience; the soldiers perched on back of the reflecting light, theatre on board ship one does not see every day.

<u>Sunday Dec. 20</u>th. This has been our third calm beautiful Sunday on the water. The Chaplain held services again at 10:30 in the saloon then this afternoon he had services for the soldiers down stairs, and we who sing in the choir went down there to sing. We only have two books and glad I am that I learned the words of most of the Gospel Hymns in Rito Alto Church long ago. It seems strange now to find so many people who do not know those old hymns, especially people of my own age and younger.

It is getting warmer all the time and we keep the electric fans going. We have lost so much time it is hard to think what time it is at home now, but I suppose being 5p.m. here is about 3 o'clock in the morning there. You will be getting up after awhile to build the fires in the cold about the time we sailors got to bed. Eloise must be at home by this time or will be in a few days. We dread to think of being on board Christmas Day.

<u>Monday, Dec. 21st</u>: We had a hop on the spare deck of the boat tonight on the soldier's beck and the band played up on the bridge afterwards. One of the Lieutenants took another girl and me out as far as we could go on the point-bridge where we could see the phosphorescent light in the wake and every wave seemed to be on fire.

<u>Tuesday, Dec. 22nd</u>, We made our last trip to the baggage room today and fixed things for disembarking next Monday. The violinist played for us up on deck tonight—everybody was out and it is so hot the babies are all breaking out with prickly rash.

There are all nationalities working on this boat, one Porto Rican boy, several Philippines, Germans, Irish and Englishmen, and George, the big colored bath room steward, who has much trouble getting baths ready for all these people every day. By the way, he used to live in Denver and he is very careful to treat us right because we are Denverites.

<u>Wednesday Dec. 23rd</u>: At daylight this morning we were very near the island Guam.

It is the prettiest place we have seen yet, so green and surf dashing high on rocks and breaking into white foam on the long beach. Just after breakfast the Marines three boats full were rowed over from the land and taken on board, some of the men had been on the Island five years and it was a glad shout they gave when they stepped on board the transport. The gang plank, as kind of fire escape looking stair arrangement, was lowered from our boat and the man came up fast as they could with their guns and knapsacks. Then the boats were sent back with fresh marines from our boat and as usual at parting the band played "Auld Lang Syne" and <u>those</u> men don't look happy over their change. Our whole attention was held by the natives from land who kept coming up in small boats to sell fruit, shells, and baskets, some of the passengers lowered ropes and strings down to the boats and had the ware tied on to pull up and dropped the money down, while others lowered buckets down and had them filled with coconuts and bananas. The bananas are little short things and so good with a sour taste one can hardly recognize they are bananas. We took some pictures of the native boats and the big rocks that should prove very interesting. The native oranges are green and are surely not very good because we saw some big boxes sent from the boat over with the men. We all wanted to go ashore so much and explore a little, but passengers are not allowed to land any more, since some teachers got left there and once even the Quartermaster was left. This has been the hottest—it is even nearer the equator here than where we will be in the P.I.

Nearly everyone is complaining dreadfully their clothes get so wet with perspiration, but I don't mind it much and can sleep all night no matter how hot the nights are. My feet hurt, so I feel like going barefoot. Nearly everyone is having an awful time trying to get their shoes on that were in another climate the right size. The sailors all wear white canvas suits now and the officers wear all white for dress. We left Guam early in the afternoon and everyone is glad because that will put us in Manila sooner.

Dec. 24th: Transport Logan, Everyone is getting ready for Christmas today. There was a Mother's meeting held in the Colonel's wife's room to arrange things for the children and of course Mabel was in attendance and will have the baby's tiny socks hung up with the others. One of the ladies has a little folding Christmas Tree that will be displayed tomorrow morning for all the children on the boat. The Musicians for the Yule Tide Music want me to go down and practice with their choir so I must stop with a Merry Christmas to all and to all a good night!!

Christmas Day Dec. 25, 1903 This has been a great day. The children's stockings were filled and they are all going around now eating candy and nuts and showing their toys. There are fourteen children ranging in age from Dorothy the youngest to some boys twelve years old and they were delightfully surprised when they were ushered into the smoking room where they hung their stockings; to find the room all brilliant with light and decorated with flags and banners, then the little Christmas Tree, and in the middle of the room a Palm Tree. It was decorated with strings of cranberries and kindergarten paper chains, bags of candy, boxes of nuts, and dolls. The room was all festooned with magnolia flowers that were brought from Guam a few days ago. When they saw the children's glee, I think the men were not sorry they had given up their smoking room. The Chaplain held service out on the soldier deck this morning and we sang out there accompanied by an organ and violin. We had songs from the Episcopal Hymnal this time and closed with "My Country 'Tis of Thee". The Chaplain likened the story of our Savior's birth with the birth of the American Flag, and showed why we hold every birthday sacred, and this one greatest gift day sets the example for us keeping the anniversaries. He spoke of the little house in Philadelphia still standing that was where Betsy Ross made the first banner of the stars and stripes near the place where Benjamin Franklin is buried in the old Quaker burial ground. There was a band concert of devotional music in the morning and another concert of lighter strains in the afternoon, closed by the Midway Plaisance(sp?) piece, it was played well and it seemed like that day we went down the Midway and laughed ourselves nearly sick over the songs, dances, and shoutings on either side. A real Christmas dinner and another band concert wound up the day, then a crowd of us came to the dining room and had salad, sandwiches, sherbet, and cake. By that time the mothers were having their celebration trying to get the children to sleep after so much Christmas.

<u>Saturday, December 26th</u>: The old year is on its home run and we expect to greet the New Year in a new land. We saw a rainbow this morning. I hope the sailors noticed it—if the saying is true "rainbow at night is the sailors delight and a rainbow in the morning a sailors warning". White caps are big again and the boat is rolling so that the people who came on at Guam are seasick.

<u>Sunday Dec. 27th</u>: We are in the straits this morning with land on both sides, we are going slow so as not to reach Manila before morning, but it is raining so we can only see the sea and I am dreadfully disappointed not to see the volcanoes on this end of the island near Begashi where Mabel lived before. We have seen a good

many porpoises this morning, they are a great big fish and look like shark but they swim out of the water with a rotary motion. It seems strange that we are really reaching the stopping place; it seems as if we have lived on this boat always. Raining harder than ever, the children are barefoot running around deck playing in the water. It seems far from home out here where the Islands are on one side and I suppose China is out there not so awfully far off to the west. Now I begin to wish that February would hurry and come so we can get some mail because the only nice thing about being away from home is to get home letters. This is supposed to the dry season but it has poured all day and we are afraid we can't wear our white dresses ashore, after all our dark dresses will have to be resurrected from the trunks.

Dec. 28th: Monday morning, Manila Bay. We anchored at last, but quarantined, some cases of mumps and chicken pox on board. The quarantine officer has sent for another doctor so it will only be a few hours till they let most of us off we think. Lou is outside, in a little launch and Mabel is having a fit nearly because they can't get near enough to talk. 4p.m. It was all a fairy story; they have sent us back to the Quarantine station, 25 miles away to the Island of Maracilles. We don't like the indefinite delay but will see a good deal of the Islands.

Dec. 29, 1903. Maracilles Transport began. To be quarantined is not altogether dreadful when people have no greater inconvenience than we first class passengers have these two days. Our only hardship is that Maracilles is a beautiful green mountainous island and we are compelled to stay on board and only look at it from a pretty distance. Today all of us who wanted to went to the bath houses on the dock and indulged in the most luxuriant cold fresh water shower bath. It made me cool for the rest of the day. It is not nearly as warm as I expected to find the P.I. A nice breeze is blowing and the water is *quiet and it looks so nice to see the natives rowing around in canoes. There are some curious birds flying around here like hawks with white bodies and red wings.*

When we first came into dock yesterday, the soldiers were taken off a company at a time and lined up in front of the bathhouse with their guns and telescope suitcases. Each man was given an old wet gunny sack to put all his clothes into, some were wise and left their shoes with their hats and gloves in their valises, others put everything in to be steamed. It was quite a study in human nature to us so we watched (rubbered at) them from the deck. Some men carefully sorted things and carefully weighed the problem of having all their treasures ruined, while others crammed everything helter skelter in on top of the blankets. Then they marched off with the sack on their shoulder in stocking feet and without coats, it was the queerest looking caravan we ever saw, they all took it seriously as if they were going to the gallows instead of to a shower bath.

The second company took it more in a joking way and the first man to step in line said "The immigrants are arriving" then another said, "This makes me think of the time we came over from Ireland". It was all a perfect farce because the things left in the valises were disinfected by Philippino boys taking a pail of long named germ killer around and giving each pile of clothes just one sprinkle with a whisk broom, it only spoiled the things on top and could not possibly have done much good. As the first-company came out they compared notes, one fellow asked if it was awfully hot and his answer was "I guess NOT, they hang an icicle around your neck," another fellow remarked when his steamed property was returned "I wish you could see my best girl's picture now". Today they stand on land and splashed around on the beach until the ship was fumigated. Mabel and the baby escaped vaccination again, but I was not slighted. 10p.m. Anchored for the night just outside Manila. We are glad of the prospect of going ashore at last since the yellow flag is lowered now. We had a hop on the star deck again tonight and all the wives are hoping even yet that their husbands will learn that we are out here and will come out in launches. Mabel and a good many other women received cablegrams today from Manila saying the transport would be expected tomorrow morning so we are ahead of time again as we have been all the time. That was the reason more than anything that we were quarantined, because we came a day sooner than expected and the Quarter Master was not ready for us. Well, I must pack again and have my letter ready for the mail tomorrow.

<u>Wednesday morning, Dec. 30th</u>. Manila Bay is as filled with boats it is like going into New York. The Hotels are all filled so we won't have a very good place to stay so will probably go to Camp Stotsenburg tomorrow. The baby is having the best kind of time pulling Lou's hair. Some of the eatables look very nice whether they are good or not. It must be terribly hard for the cooks when it is so hot and close below. I keep wondering what you are doing at home. Write me all about Eloise coming home and what Rafe and Walter are doing, whether Papa & Mama are well and all about yourself. How many times I have wished you could be with me, we can have such good times sightseeing together can't we. When I left, Mrs. Garretson gave me the little opal pin that Ralph always wore. The cockroaches are simply awful and spoil things too, make musty spots on white goods, of course, my pretty cushion had to have that stain, but they don't bite so we are fortunate. You never saw me so white before, about three shades of tan have disappeared and I weigh nearly 125 lbs. This is no wonder since all we have to do is eat and sleep. Dorothy is so well, and so much easier to take care of, she is getting curious now. 12 O'clock Wednesday, safe on land again at the old hotel 77 Calle Real we are going out to drive in a Victoria on the luretta.

Wednesday Dec. 30th: Manila P.I. We are all safe on Manila just as well as we can be. I am so glad I came, everything is so strange and the people are so queer. Wish I knew some Spanish, as it is I am lost when out of sight of Lou and Mabel. We go to Stotsenburg day after tomorrow, Jan 1st. We must see what we can of the city in a short time so I close and will write to Papa before we leave so it will go on our returning transport. I wish you could have such nice warm weather now, it is not too hot.

Love to you all, Bess

The leather-bound diary of Bess's trip continues:

Camp Stotsenburg, Manila, Philippine Islands. I helped set up the Ball's garrison home. Many visitors at Camp come calling. All of the officers and families visit the new families who arrive.

January 5, 1904: I got my room and mosquito netting set up. I remodeled my blue silk dress for dinner and my old white dress for "Hops". The whole regiment was on parade today in back of the officer's quarters. We went out to see it. The old cavalry horses are beautiful and prance to the music. I found an interesting article: "One of the most unique little railways in the world runs from Manila to Dagupan, in the island of Luzon. Every tie under its rails is made of mahogany." I hope to see that! Social life is fine. Lieutenants escort us to the balls and several invitations have come to go horseback riding. Watching baseball games is another pastime. I borrowed a friend's divided skirt for riding. The Lt. (Ball) is often on guard duty and I keep Mabel and the baby company.

January 24th, 1904: A picnic party was planned and Lt. Deitrick asked me and because he is Lou's friend, I thought it best to go, even if it is Sunday—I did not enjoy the trip so will go to church the next time!! Mrs. Whitmore chaperoned and we went five miles up the Ban Ban River on horseback with lunch. Mr. Low, Miss Hatfield, Lt. Davidson, Miss Kerber, Lt. Deitrick and myself were the party. We saw beautiful trees, ferns and begonias growing wild on the rocks with tall holly ferns and wandering jew.

We camped for lunch by the Ban Ban river which was walled on each side by high rocks and bamboo. Lt. Deitrick tried to walk over the bridge and it broke where the Negritos had cut it. Mr. D. fell thirty feet to the water, then twenty feet under and was not hurt, but swam out of the whirlpool to the bank. I was glad to get home that evening.

Monday: A RED LETTER DAY as my first news from home, a letter from Dollie, came this afternoon. All was well on Dec. 14th. Mail came by way of China.

February 1, 1904: Just a month ago, we took up our habitation here and much of military life has been instilled in me. So far, I think it is far too idle a life to be ideal for women. Today I was told that I was a good influence in the camp. Would that I could believe that I am an influence of good anywhere. I find the army men not entirely to my liking. They don't care to talk books, or fashion, or show how intellectual they can be, but conversations are on nonsense. I have made friends of numerous delightful ladies, made small trips by carriage & horseback around the islands & to Manila, enjoyed the social schedule and some discussions with women on books, sewing, fashion, and world affairs.

Lt. Deitrick, Chaplain Miller, and Lt. Bull became frequent callers for riding, dances, concerts, and picnics. I care for the baby frequently so Mabel can go with her husband, when he is off duty, to affairs they enjoy. This has been an altogether enlightening experience.

March 15, 1904: The telegraph came granting passage in the Transit "Kilpatrick" back to the U.S. by way of the Suez Canal.

March 24th: *My last day of garrison life. Made all my calls for good-byes, packed up, then went out for a horseback ride with Helen and Chaplain Miller. We went to the river and got my riding skirt wet, so I couldn't pack it to take home. In the evening I went with Mabel and Mr. Deitrick to the entertainment. Came home and several officers were waiting to say goodbye to me. Chaplain gave me a hymnal with music for use on the boat going home. I departed for Manila March 25th with Chaperone, Miss Daisy Hubbell on the Transport "Kilpatrick", bound for home.*

March 28th: *Out on the China Sea. Exercising, sewing, & cards keep us busy on board. We went through the Malacca Straits and on 3/31 are off Singapore. We spent Good Friday in Singapore Harbor and had a most unusual Easter in the Straits of Malacca. Half of the passengers are ill from shore food in Singapore, but the sea is perfectly smooth. Miss Koerper and I started reading "The Light That Failed" aloud, but the day seemed awfully long. I tried in the p.m. to rally a group to sing Christian songs, but all were too lazy or tired. It was very discouraging to try to do my Christian duty & fail.*

April 4, 1904: *We're sailing the Bay of Bengal. The day began with a Lieutenant. We had a very good lesson and watched a beautiful sunset. By tomorrow we will be past any site of land. I have been playing Whist with several passengers.*

April 5th *We awoke to find very rough seas, many are ill & I had to dismiss my class abruptly and was seasick for the first time in my life.*

Out on the Indian Ocean, typhoon type winds are allowing us to make only 7 miles per day. Odd to have to get out cap & cape due to cold. We thought the Indian Ocean would be mild. My class is still half sick and cross. I walked the deck in the p.m. and read "Buell Hampton", who says the following: "Marriage is a mystery --------awakening an introduction to the real, where happiness of each hangs upon the caprice of both."

Fourth day on the Indian Ocean—we will reach Colombo tomorrow. We had a celebrative dinner of sirloin roast with mushrooms, turkey with cranberry sauce, beans and spinach, boiled beets, asparagus with mayonnaise, ice cream and pudding. I wore my old lilac dress!

April 8th: We are rounding the point of the Island of Colon and we are reading up on all we see. I've been busy with laundry, washing hair, and writing letters to post from land. We anchored at noon on April 9th at Colombo Harbor, met by a mob of native divers—the noisiest savage-looking set I've ever seen, rowing in log rafts. Mrs. Wilcox and I went in a carriage to Galle Fall Hotel, a beautiful beach drive. We stopped in some museums, had dinner on the gardens, and bought mangos (unlike Philippine Island mangos) which were green instead of yellow. We listened to the band from Battleship Kentucky in the harbor then took a rickshaw back to the hotel and a concert in the illuminated gardens. Sunday we went to a native Catholic Church where natives come in bedecked with jewels.
We then went to a beautiful English Church and were invited to tea and tour on the "Man of War" British ship "Porpoise". The commanding officer gave me some brass buttons.

April 11th: Back on the 'Kilpatrick' it seems like home. We were entertained by jewel peddlers and bought two ruby and pearl rings for $17. Set sail at 4:20 p.m. to cross Persian Gulf to Aden.

April 12th: We are on the Arabian Sea, making 11 knots per hour. The Kentucky passed us at 15 knots per hour. The sea is like a mirror! People bother me so dreadfully some times. Usually I can be very charitable toward conditions but when, as today, I go off to some quiet part of the deck to read up on history, and really learn something, immediately someone comes and talks about nothing. I have to be polite and talk, too, then I find another place and again someone talks—I lost my patience entirely.

We are 8 days on the Arabian Sea. At night the mirror smooth sea is filled with phosphorescent-like miniature fireworks coming from the ocean depths.

My teaching of the children each day includes reading, sewing, and encouraging singing. I try encouraging the adults to sing hymns, read and play games. We cast anchor in the inner harbor of the gulf of Aden—barren rocks, sea gulls, and the weirdest island I've seen. Hawkers came to the boat with ostrich feathers, coral, and baskets. On shore, we saw Jews, Arabs, and Somali people. We set sail again through Straits of Babel—Massdele. I sketched as we saw Africa on one side and Asia on the other. Entering the Red Sea, temperate zone, it is much colder. A new friend, Mrs. Harrison, asked me to tour Cairo with her. I wish she were my chaperone. We deposited $20 for the Cairo trip.

<u>April 25th</u>: SUEZ CANAL We were all ready to start for Cairo when quarantine officers came on board and warned of plague in Suez. We were not allowed to buy anything. The water around Suez was more blue than any other place. We saw camel caravans and fishing junks, all numbered on their sails. I saw the place where the Israelites crossed into Canaan and Moses' wells.

We started through the canal about dark and had right of way until 12 p.m., then had to tie up many times for others to pass. Now we are out on the Mediterranean Sea (4 days). Steaming along yet another sea that looks just like the others, only it is cold and a stiff breeze blowing. At Port Sard, "Wickedest Port in the World", our Pilots went ashore but we were not allowed to land. It was very disappointing, but there are plague regulations. Tin casting guards were placed on the ropes of every ship to repel rats. The Mediterranean is *deep blue but we nearly froze out on deck. Seas are rough and many are ill again. On April 30th we came in sight of land and steamed into Malta Harbor. This port has tier after tier of walls, a huge fortification. Mrs. Harrison, Mrs. LaPier, Miss Koerper, and I went ashore in little gondolas and hired a yellow covered hearse-like carriage to drive through Grand Victoria Gate to the Armory. Here we saw Napoleons coach. We bought some nice maltan lace in both silk and linen and a coral necklace. We went to see "The Gay Parisian" in the evening at the Marvorel Theater. Here we had little boxes where we had to look straight ahead out holes in the wall at the stage. British soldiers in boxes above us passed their bottle around and shouted.*

Sunday in Malta we visited the San Dominican and St. Paul's Churches in Valetta, then went to mass at the historic St. John's Church As we drove through the streets we saw vendors selling to church goers---shoe & tailor materials to hot buns and candies. God has been very good to me to make my life so full. I am so happy and have such an opportunity to see what I have longed to see. I trust that I may do something to make myself worthy to a slight degree at least. I went with Miss Koerper, Lieutenant and Mrs. Game to St. John's Church and the Chapel of Bones again this morning. After church I bought a cameo brooch and a painting of a Madonna. In the afternoon Mr. Werts took me for a drive, we picked the red poppies from the rye fields, and old women gave us some roses that I sketched in the evening. Later we went back ashore and I bought a black lace collar and some sliver beads and Maltese cross.

May 3rd: We lifted anchor and left Malta, the place I have had one of the happiest times of my life. I've made sketches that several aboard have asked me to copy for them. I have a new roommate, who is always getting sea sick. I have been reading history of Malta and how St. Paul was shipwrecked there in 58 a.d.

Gibraltar: They would not let us ashore since the Kentucky was ahead of us and British Fleet expected soon, and there was not room for us all in port. Gale strength cold winds are blowing with long wait ahead, so we went ashore in a little sailboat that seemed ready to capsize at any moment. We found a little carriage as we had in Malta, to do a little shopping and survey the towns and Victoria Gardens.

I bought a long Spanish Lace Matilla for $2.50 that was priced at $7.50, a miniature jewel box, and a belt. We saw an equestrian show, cricket, and a polo game. Sunday I made some sketches then went to lunch with Mrs. LaPere and to church at and English Cathedral. It seemed more lovely and home-like than anything since I left Denver in November. After church we went for a drive to see galleries, the tunnels, and the most beautiful views I have ever seen, with blue Mediterranean on the East and the Straits and Africa on the other side. It is certainly the strongest point in the world. Through the Straits of Gibraltar we saw whales and a great school of porpoise. Sketching and card games keep us busy.

May 10th: Atlantic Ocean (13 days) It is cold and damp and the water filled with red jellyfish. I visited the Captain's Quarters, the bridge, and am to tour the "hospital" tomorrow. Weather is worse and many are seasick. During the night, a wave went over the upper decks and all of the rooms were wet on our side. My clothing was all damp. One of 'my children', little Octavia, has pneumonia and her mother is dreadfully worried. We're now wishing the trip were over. The Atlantic always looks black and cold. I'm busy painting dinner cards, with scenes we've seen. Octavia is better. The ship is being painted and people fall against the wet paint when the ship rolls. It's miserably cold.

May 14th: We've had a lovely social of cards and music and last night two of us played music until midnight. I'm anxious to know how all is at home. I began packing for New York.

May 18th: We have been in the Gulf Stream and we're off Newfoundland Banks. It's warmer, but continues to rain. My chaperone, Mrs. Harrison, fell on the wet deck and had to have 5 stitches in her head. As we near New York we see more ships. I'm sketching Coney Island and the harbor as we approach. Everyone is very excited. I was blue that all wouldn't be well at home and no one would meet me, but I was pleasantly surprised with a letter that all is well and a friend from home was first to meet us.

Grand Hotel, New York City, I stayed with Mrs. Harrison for a few days of sightseeing. Father will meet me in Ohio, with Mother & Eloise joining us for the Exposition. In New York I visited galleries, saw plays, toured Belleview Hospital & almost missed the ferry to the Railroad at Penn Station. In Philadelphia, Gertrude and Garrett and their darling 2 yr. old met me and I went to their home in Camden, New Jersey. I enjoyed showing them my souvenirs. I spent Decoration Day in Camden, New Jersey—different parades, music, & events than I am used to at home. Father was detained at home and didn't meet me in Ohio, but my Aunt Mary met and took me to her home in Yellow Springs, Ohio. I went to the St. Louis World's Fair with cousins, then back home to Denver and Aunt Lizzie's.

A family folktale existed about Bess's love life. It was heard that "Bess never married because two suitors had a duel and shot each other and she never found love again!" The article found in a diary does indicate two officers from the time of her visit did indeed meet a violent death. No mention was made in the diary or in future letters of any connection to these gentlemen in her life. The article being carefully saved does indicate these were important people in her journey. The documented incident occurred several months after Bess returned home. Her friend Mabel must have sent her the article. It stated (with date, *"Oct. 1904,"* in Bess's writing):

DOUBLE TRAGEDY IN ARMY BARRACKS IN MANILA

"A cablegram was received at army headquarters yesterday announcing a double tragedy in Manila. Yesterday morning in a temporary fit of insanity, Lieutenant William D. Pritchard of the Thirteenth cavalry, stationed at Camp Stotsenberg, manila shot and killed instatly Lieutenant Fred L. Deen, aslo second lieutenant in the Thirteenth calvary. Lieutenant Pritchard then shot himself, dying instantly. Lieutenant Pritchard held an honorable military record and was appointed from North Carolina. He served in the United States Infantry at Porto Rico as second lieutenant of the cavalry in which he held a permanent appointment since June, 1902. Lieutenant Deen was appointed from Texas. No explanation or particulars were given. It is supposed the suicide was suffering from mental aberration induced by the climate."

Bess kept house for her father before and after this world round-trip November 1903 to July 1904. As Bess became restless in Colorado, she examined her interests and passions. The death of Ralph Garretson had made such an indelible mark on her life and emotions. Her goals as a teenager had been to be worldly, educated, and an interesting wife and mother. As she contemplated the premature death of her true love Ralph, she felt a strong desire to make a difference in the world in other ways. The research she had done on appendectomies and health care led her to believe Ralph's death was unnecessary if improved medical asepsis and educational methods had been enforced. This led her to the decision to become a trained professional nurse.

She researched and wrote letters to numerous schools of nursing, finally deciding on Bellevue Hospital Training School in New York City. Her world travels and expanded outlook from her experiences had opened her world far beyond the Rito Alto ranch in Moffat, Colorado.

Bess had maintained her friendship with Mr. and Mrs. Garretson, from Saluda, Colorado, visiting them often during the time she was in the San Luis Valley. The Garretsons supported her decision to pursue a nursing career and put her back in touch with their friend Major Swither, who wrote a letter of recommendation to Bellevue Hospital, in June of 1905, for Bess to begin her hospital training program to become a professional nurse.

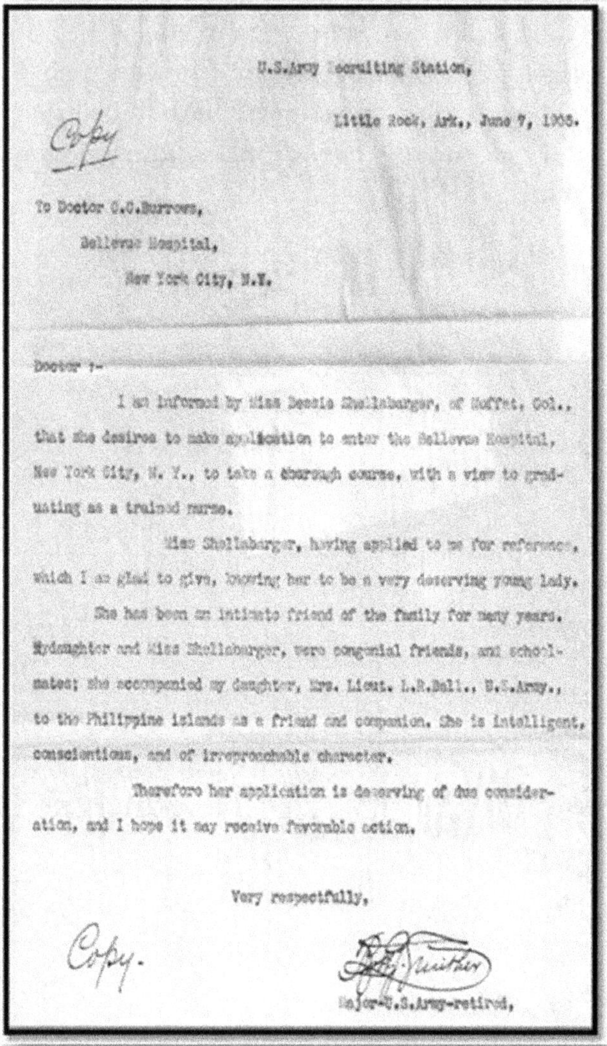

U.S.Army Recruiting Station,

Little Rock, Ark., June 7, 1906.

Copy

To Doctor G.C.Burrows,

Bellevue Hospital,

New York City, N.Y.

Doctor :-

I am informed by Miss Bessie Shellabarger, of Moffat, Col., that she desires to make application to enter the Bellevue Hospital, New York City, N. Y., to take a thorough course, with a view to graduating as a trained nurse.

Miss Shellabarger, having applied to me for reference, which I am glad to give, knowing her to be a very deserving young lady.

She has been an intimate friend of the family for many years. Mydaughter and Miss Shellabarger, were congenial friends, and school-mates; she accompanied my daughter, Mrs. Lieut. L.R.Ball., U.S.Army., to the Philippine islands as a friend and companion. She is intelligent, conscientious, and of irreproachable character.

Therefore her application is deserving of due consideration, and I hope it may receive favorable action.

Very respectfully,

Copy.

[signature] Swither

Major-U.S.Army-retired,

Major Swither's recommendation letter to Bellevue

BELLEVUE

ellevue Hospital Training School for Women Nurses was a three-year training program that covered all aspects of the nursing profession. After much research of schools of nursing in the United States, this school was the choice. Bess noted that she purposely did not keep a daily diary during these three years, so as not to detract from her studies. Class and lecture notes and copious lists of patients, treatments, and doctors and professors with whom she worked were available in her files.

Jane A. Delano, who was superintendent of the Bellevue Training School, would have a profound influence on the professional life of Bess. Miss Delano's keen interest in training for professional nurses, as well as her recruiting Red Cross nurses (which Bess was to become in 1918); her emphasis on dietetics, nursing care, and instruction in rural areas; and her tireless work to improve hospital care for American servicemen were a model for Bess's career path and interests. The following letter, received by Bess, was the beginning of her application process for nursing school:

Dear Madam: —
   Your letter received, and in reply, I send you a copy of our blank form of application and circular of information.
   Will you kindly return it to me with the required letters of reference, and a personal letter stating briefly your educational

advantages, family ties, if any, religion and reasons for desiring to become a nurse.

> *Yours very truly,*
> *Jane A. Delano*
> *Supt. Training Schools*

Jane A. Delano was studied about in history-of-nursing courses of the generations of nurses following Bess. Miss Delano was a major influence in the development of nursing education and supportive nursing organizations. Her résumé included superintendent of Bellevue School of Nursing until 1909 when she was appointed superintendent of the Army Nurse Corps. A brief time following the years that she was the superintendent of the prestigious training school at Bellevue Hospital, Jane took a leave to care for her dying mother in Charlottesville, Virginia. She, like Bess, left promising career positions to care for family.

An article concerning Miss Delano was found in Bess's diary, stating,

"For so dynamic a woman, one challenge was not enough. The same year, Miss Delano was named chairman of the National Committee on Red Cross Nursing Service and worked simultaneously as president of the American Nurses Association and chairman of the board of the American Journal of Nursing. Twenty years of innovative nursing had given Miss Delano an understanding of the country's need for more trained nurses, particularly for service in isolated areas and emergencies. She urged a plan that would place responsibility for recruiting nurses for emergency service with the Red Cross entirely in the hands of nurses themselves. State and local committees were set up under her plan, which worked so well that by 1911 there were 1,300 Red Cross nurses enrolled.'

There being no diary entries of the training years, we are left with letters about the Bellevue experiences. Bess wrote to her sister, Eloise as follows:

New York
September 5, 1907

Dear Eloise,

With one of the nurses, I'm taking my afternoon having a trip up East River on the Island Hospital Boat again and the breeze is delightsome. One of my nurses borrowed my fountain pen just before I left the ward, hence this penciled letter.

The Saguache paper told of you having the Shippey's as callers recently. Last week when we had an afternoon, we had a trip through Fordham Hospital and found it so much and the nurses home so luxurious that we wanted to stay. One of our girls had a bad spell of the blues because she didn't have new clothes that she wanted and couldn't go so we went back at evening and made her dress up in her old clothes and we took her to the Martha Washington Hotel to dinner. The place is called the old maids hotel and we had the best dinner and about killed ourselves eating, then walked down Fifth Avenue and to bed. Our discouraged girl became as happy as any of us. We are just going under a portion of bridge that overhangs the river like that one that fell in at Quebec.

Sunday I went for a car ride over in Jersey with Mr. Beck then he took me to dinner, then we went to church at St. Georges'. You see I am giddy having two dinners in one week. Now I must fast for a long season and get ready for more examinations in December and I guess I'll be the Junior to graduate in the January class because there is a long gap between me and Miss McKay who came in September. All the girls between us went or were sent home. We are going in at the dock so I must close and will send a piece of N.Y. paper with Denver gossip that greeted is in Sunday's Journal.

Love to you all, Your sister Bess

A second letter was found.

The Dock
East 26 St. N.Y.
9/22/07

Dear Eloise,'

Last night I was dreaming of thee love, was dreaming"—After getting your postal that you had to wander around Alamosa alone, how I would like to have meandered about with you, but instead at that time I was in this break-neck place trying to do twice as much as I was able and manage any ward with dignity. Twenty-eight sick men needing attention all at once with only half enough nurses. Miss Burk took my best nurse away first when it was heaviest, and they surely found they had stirred up a hornet's nest because I made the biggest kind of a row to Miss Goodrich. It is the first time I've peeped in 'complaint' since Xmas, we have to let the powers here know that we are living sometimes to get fair play.

I've been across town once this last week is the extent of my doings since last chapter, so there is nothing to write. East river is very peaceful at high tide this morning and two big yachts are sentinels out here now.

Last night I answered the door when the bell rang after twelve because my room is just at the head of the stairs and right next Miss Brink's Suite and no one else seemed to respond. I found it was one of the maids come in drunk. There is a chair across the door of course and I didn't have to let her in so turned back to ask Miss Brink what to do and met her on the stairs. She talked to the girl awhile and found she was so noisy she couldn't let her in to waken the house and it seemed the maid's name is the same as mine and Miss Brink said "Now Bessie we can't let you in that way, so you must go away" It just sent a horror through me as accustomed as I am now to such things. To think how it must be to be driven away from the only place one could call home, well, Miss Brink went to the phone and called up the Hospital to send an officer to take charge of her so a big policeman took her away from where she was sprawling at the door. All the time the woman was shouting things about Miss Brink and it was two o'clock when the street was finally still. Miss Brink got quite excited over the wrong side of it, so she said "we must go up to the tea room window and see where he takes her," so we saw him escort her to the alcoholic ward and at every window on the other side of the street there was a white robed figured watching the proceedings—it was all quite exciting and I couldn't go to sleep for a long time. Well, I must run home and get ready for dinner.

The Canon City boy who is a patient in my ward is getting well now.

Love from your sister,
Bess

Another letter dated December 12, 1960, to nursing student and namesake Alice Elizabeth, who was attending University of Colorado School of Nursing in Denver, Colorado, is postmarked from 145 S. Vernon, Tempe, Arizona, and tells of the Bellevue experience:

Dear Alice Elizabeth:

Your lovely card with the grand news about capping has come just in time because I was on the point of writing you after a note from Rito Alto about the plans to be in Denver for this ceremony (only you and I know what a really victorious day the 15th will be). I've even wished to send a note to your Director of Nurses requesting her to give you my love and congratulations, but you are not so well known to her and her staff as you will be in the fall when you get the Junior Stripe. You have really been a college girl so far and that to me seems a most elevated beginning. I was amazed even in our outstanding school in 1905 there was only one college graduate and

*I the only other with even one year to my credit so you can see it was
not difficult to get good grades, we had no college graduates as teachers except the Medical Director—and (my) college was finished long
after at Columbia University.*

*Capping in those days was more individual but no less serious.
One day I was called to the office and so alarmed it was hard to open
the door--thinking I would be sent home, but instead Miss Jane A.
Delano said--"You may be excused from the ward long enough to go
over to the Home to make your cap, the House Mother will give you
the material and instructions". "Thank you" came right from my
heart and pride gave me a lift. I think just what we need in nursing is to approach the dignity of our General Miss Delano and the
understanding human kindness of the brilliant Miss A.W. Goodrich
who signed my diploma after Miss Delano had gone to organize
Army Nursing. My diploma hangs at the Wales, Otis ranch.*

Love and my blessing, Aunt B.

Bess wrote in her 1963 diary the following note that tells of the importance of her Bellevue cap:

*Received invitation from precious grand-niece, Alice Elizabeth
Selch, asking me to attend her capping ceremony at the University
of Colorado School of Nursing. I will not be able to attend, but I
wrote to Alice congratulating her on this special time in her professional progress.*

*My capping was an auspicious time for me. I was summoned
from floor duty to the office of Supt. Delano in the middle of the
day. Fearing I had done something terribly wrong and would be
dismissed, I was fairly trembling as I knocked on her door. After
welcoming me, she handed me a packet of fabric, telling me I was
relieved from duty for the afternoon, to return to the nurse's quarters and stitch my cap. The house mother would have pattern and*

instructions and help me complete this project and I was to wear the cap the next day to duty.

(Author's note: The Bellevue cap, on display at the Saguache County Museum, is a complicated, delicate work. It is a sheer cotton fabric, gathered in a "dust cap" pattern. Until the late twentieth century, a nurse's cap was her "crown," indicating her school and her status.)

Bess wrote another letter to her aunt Lizzie, written on "Continuation of History and Bedside Notes" paper (obviously while on duty), dated April 19, 1908. There is uncertainty about dates, since the program from *"Graduating Exercises of the Training Schools connected with Bellevue and Allied Hospitals"* is dated April 9 and states *"Graduating Class of 1907."* It is not clear whether the previous letter was written after her graduation or if graduation was, indeed, in April 1908. Completing the three-year program would make that a certainty. She graduated highest in her class.

Dear Aunt Lizzie;

The present has kept me so busy there hasn't been even a chance to write home an account of my commencement, so you will be first since I couldn't get only this piece of invitation extra and I sent most of the whole ones to people I thought would come.

We hurried home from duty that night at 7:30 and found the dining room all cleared of chairs and tables for dancing so we only had bread and cheese for dinner, then put on our best stiff uniforms with cap and aprons and went to Cornell Medical College across First Ave. where we formed in line with the men nurses who were all in white. We sat in the front seats while our guests had the back of the auditorium. We listened to the addresses then filed down to get our diplomas and pins. When all the girls were getting boxes of flowers and seeking friends, I felt like in a strange land, as I did when coming to this place, until I found waiting for me Miss May Gardner, Ella Wales' daughter, Miss Dunlap and Mr. Beck.

Then we went back to the home and danced and ate good things, but there was such a crush in the halls we could hardly turn. It was all a grand success but most of us were tired out and I'm all used up yet, so they have made me head nurse down here in the baby tent where it is easy, because next week when I finish I expect to take a pretty hard position that will be a good deal of walking, but it will not be bad. Our Superintendent asked me to take the place of a retiring Assistant Supervisor of the Training School and after much debate I decided to take it because such a good chance will not come again soon and it will give me a name for other Institutional work. The place quite terrifies me because I will teach two classes and follow the nurses up in the wards and see that they carry on the work.

I'm to have a vacation of one month the last of June, and can't think how that will be enough time to visit at home, so I'm afraid you will have to take a shorter visit from me this time, then in the future we can have that long visit but just at present there is so much to do in this world we must all keep busy. We all work here as hard as we can and yet so many poor patients don't get the proper care. In my new work there will be very little real nursing, except looking after the sick nurses, but I dislike looking after disciplining the younger nurses, when some of us have just been working together, but yet it is a shame to spend three years here then not make any use of what I've learned. I do so long to stay at home. I just hope they will not do a bit of entertaining while I am at home and all the time be taken up with company, because I'm going to be jealous and want all their time for myself.

Miss Gardner seems like a very nice girl, I'm going out to Staten Island some day to see her. Last night I was entertained in a small way at a friend's home here, she is an older nurse whom I became acquainted with through a mutual acquaintance who nurses in the Philippines. So many people are inviting me here and there now because they think I'm soon leaving for the west, but I'm glad to find I have a few friends here. It is not like the West where one can believe people much. My head doctor just now is a Western man and it is such a relief to talk with him, he tells all about his wife and family, his aims, and discusses everything in general just as we all do out home, instead of cussing some particular unfortunate. I'm afraid they will find me entirely too liberal for an Assistant Supt. because I believe in people having a few ideas of their own and not doing a certain way just because someone else did, then I think this place would be less hard to take a training in if we could be treated as if possessing minds! One of the doctors spoke well when he said, 'if he hated any one very much and had a particular grudge against her, he would want her to enter Bellevue Training School,' yet many of us live through it and are dunces enough to stay afterwards, but then there is the new Hospital in view and the new home.

Well, I couldn't finish this in the ward even if the work was light with only nice babies while we are quarantined for measles, so I've been writing this Easter night in my room while a lot of the girls have been in to tease me about putting on White Uniforms next week and sitting at the big table in the dining room. With it all I'm quite flustered and mad and wish they would hush because it's hard enough to go into anyhow. Isn't it strange how care-free we nurses are off duty, where there tonight I leave my little sick babies with a new nurse and don't worry at all and I may find one gone in the morning. They are just too dear yet some are mere skeletons, but it is so good when they begin to pick up and gain. I had planned to go home via Galveston by boat, but now will hurry across country as fast as possible and must keep on the lookout for excursion rates. I guess the Democratic Convention is too late for me. You see I'm getting out early and my time is up April 25th because there is so much vacation time coming to us we couldn't get when needed. I've only had the two weeks in three years.

You must forgive me for writing only of self, but we have little in common now since people and times have so changed since we were together. But soon I'm sure I'll blow into the good old country again *and will cast about for a man to marry, settle down to a happy ever after and let the nurses take care of themselves. Now it is time for lights to be out so love me a little even if I make you a short visit.*

Love to you all, Your niece, Bess

P.S. Let Eloise see this since I've not written to the dear child for weeks. I've been very negligent and went to church only once over at the chapel this Easter and have slept all this afternoon off duty. But, we have been going so much lately we are all tired out, we had a box at the opera given to part of the class and that was so good.

A final letter about the Bellevue years was written to her mother as she completed her course of study:

Dear Mother,

Well I've accepted the position and will step into it April 25th in White Uniform, but it seems as if the bottom had fallen out of everything. My plans are so upset and I want to go home, but then a nurse can never do as she likes. Dollie seems to misunderstand about my vacation it does not come until the last of June after the examinations. Miss Goodrich offered it to me now that is to begin 25, and last till May 25 but I want it when Eloise is at home and the weather is nice and there is not so much work with the cattle. Of course I'll take the quickest train instead of a boat and will not stop to see anyone, only about a day with Aunt Lizzie because my time at home will be so short and I must make Rafe and Blanche a little visit, but I am going to ride and drive around with a Mr. A. Shellabarger most of the time so if the rest of you want to see me you will have to go with us too, and we must have a camp fire/picnic up at the canyon one day too. Miss Brink is very good to me in letting me finish up any time at the baby tent where it is not hard and I love the babies so much even if they are sick and scrawny. That lovely commencement gift from you and Dollie is going to buy for me a *pair of shell side combs, you will think I'm awfully extravagant, but that is what I want and I'm going now to Macy's to get them. I have my spring suit and hat and most of my uniforms so will not want more than $25.00 because I'll be earning soon though my third month's pay will not come to me until after the first of July.*

I'm so glad Walter is better and hope he will be all right and not have to diet so long as I have. Even yesterday that itching came back to my skin and I had to stop eating anything sweet to allay it. We must have the same kind of livers, as we have the same hay fever.

Last week I was just about worked to death, was on Friday night until after twelve as Night Supervisor after working in the day, then Saturday night was up until 2:30 in the operating room again so that yesterday forenoon when I was off and intended going to some nice church, I didn't wake up until I was late going on duty at noon. Now I have my afternoon on Monday and I'm drying my washed hair in a flood of sunshine that invades my room, so you see I'm cleaning up for commencement and we girls have been fixing our aprons and uniforms until we shall be fit for 'spotless town'. The only thing I hope I'll not get so shaky in the knees when I go up to get my diploma as I did in High School.

A funny postal came from Crestone and I can't imagine from whom unless from Mrs. Frazee. Well I must hustle about or the stores will be closed. Let me tell you something consoling, I'm going to chain a dictionary to myself when I get to teaching and also try not to make too many breaks in Grammar. Tell Dollie I'm going to bring a trunk full of cap material home for her to make up a supply for me because my patience will be tried to the utmost teaching each new class to make caps.

Love to you all, Bess

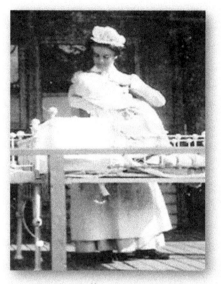

Bess in Bellevue Nursery as
Student Nurse

Bess caring for niece Emma and
nephew William at home on the
ranch. Wearing graduate uniform

THE PROFESSIONAL YEARS: 1908–1918

"To be a nurse is to walk with God, along the path that the Master trod," wrote Florence Nightingale. This philosophy shaped the actions and professional conscience of Bess. The call of family and the West were also a motivational force for her journey. Bess went home to Rito Alto for a brief vacation, returning to Bellevue Hospital for her appointment as junior supervisor and instructor in Maternal Medicine. This she found to be a valuable experience, but after a few months, she was offered a better position as assistant directress at Touro Infirmary in New Orleans. She accepted this move as more adventure and had one hundred students in her care, beginning her long history of educating new nurses.

The Touro Infirmary history on the hospital archive website fills us in on its past:

Established in 1990, the Touro Infirmary Archives houses founding records dating from the hospital's incorporation after Touro's death in 1854 and the acceptance of the hospital by directors named in his will. "I give and bequeath to found the "Hebrew Hospital of New Orleans" the said contemplated Hospital to be organized according to law, as a charitable Institution for the relief of the Indigent sick, by my Executors and such other persons as they may associate with them conformably with the law of Louisiana." The struggles to keep the fledgling hospital open through reconstruction, bank crashes, panics and wars is chronicled in minutes and annual reports of the Board of Directors/ Managers/ Trustees which continue in an almost unbroken series to the present. Two admission books record every patient who entered the hospital during the years 1855-1860 and 1869-1891. Of particular interest to researchers, these books record the patient's name, place of birth, age, sex, diagnosis and treatment, and financial charges.

Each patient's entry also includes the last place he or she visited before coming to New Orleans, which has been of great interest in tracing the spread of disease such as cholera and yellow fever. For those researching African-American heritage and history, the many entries for slaves, which also contain the name of the financially responsible party (owner or slave trader), have been of great interest. Although these two books contain patient names, in general the archives does not collect patient records or personnel records. The archives also contains materials relating to Touro's role in medical history, which includes, among others, early leadership in the field of hemodialysis, insulin research, and nuclear medicine and rehabilitation. Built on a tradition of excellent care, community involvement and faith, Touro continues to maintain its role as a vital institution for healthcare in our city.

In 1910, Bess was called home to Rito Alto because of illness in the family. There seemed to be a pattern of responding to family and quitting jobs to become the family caregiver. During this stay "at home," she received a packet of letters from Dr. Dudley Conley. The packet of half-page letters contained the thoughts of a love-struck surgical resident in New York. This romance had never surfaced until the folded packet of letters dropped out of one of the sketchpads Bess had saved among the diaries. It is apparent that Bess and Dr. Conley were not completely of like mind. Bess had her professional goals firmly planned out with service to others as her focus, while Dr. Conley loved her but felt he could not support a wife on a resident's salary and his goals were less firmly defined. This relationship unfolded as follows:

February 11, 1910
Dudley S. Conley, M.D.
342 West 56th Street, New York

My dear Bess—

I hardly know how to advise you about your position but if you have a good place offered to you out there I can't see why you should wish to come back to Belleview or to New York. You know none of us in this city really exist and sometimes existence is pretty hard. Bess, I'm sorry I ever wrote you as I did once upon a time. Had I known how this medical game was going to work, I should have kept my feelings to myself. But of course, I thought I should soon be rich. Not that I'm discouraged, for I am doing better than most of those who started with me, but I find that expenses are so big here that I am barely able to keep going even in the very modest establishment which I maintain. So anything like marriage must be put away from me. Rather hard to write such things, but to say I never supposed I could love anyone. For so much in fact to ask you to share the uncertainty of my career. For it is uncertain even now tho I am beginning to do pretty well. But I often stop and wonder just when the bottom the bottom will drop out and I shall be left high and dry. Thank you for the leaves, they suggest the big West, the forests, the purity of life, and most of all your own dear self. And here am I cooped up in this great big selfish city. Don't think about letters, Bess. You know I'm the worst yet in that line. Only this morning I had a letter from my mother reminding me I had not written home for several weeks. And so you and Dr. Wall are corresponding.
Don't stop, but be very careful what you write. Personally I have always pitied him rather than disliked him. But I would not trust him for an instant, anything else would be a greater mistake. Good bye, dearest, until next time. But don't count letters and you wouldn't if you knew how I prize any word from you. It has been awfully good of you to keep on writing and it is just like the dear girl I have

always known. Sometime you must get terribly cross with me don't you! I should not blame you a bit. But go on and write won't you? Maybe I'll improve some day.

Fondly as ever, Dud

[No date included, but this is the next in the packet of letters:]

Dudley S. Conley, M.D.
342 West 56th Street, New York

Dearest Bess—

Your letter received yesterday. It is awfully good of you to write to such a poor correspondent but am glad you understand. I hardly know how to advise you in regard to the position which has been of-fered to you but to me it seems a pretty good offer. I am sure you like institutional work much more that you would private Nursing. You are so much more independent.

The life of a private Nurse is pretty hard it seems to me. Of course it would be fine to have you in New York but even than you would be so busy that I would get to see you very seldom. All of the girls from Bellevue seem to have a cast most of the time. Now Bess, I want you to forget what I have said about Dr. Wall.

What I have told you is simply my opinion and when I am still of the same way of thinking yet I don't want to influence you any way or the other. I think it is a pretty safe rule in this life to take people as they are to you. If he is a good friend to you and is square with you, why be the same with him and don't let anyone influence you. As a matter of fact he could tell you much worse things about me than I would of him for I've never been an angel and probably never will be.

I wrote you a letter two weeks ago, kept it two days, then tore it up. It was entirely too foolish. I knew you would be disgusted. But had I known I was to lose a box of good things by not sending it, perhaps I should have chanced it. Write and let me know about the position.

Write often anyway. I don't hear from you nearly often as I should like.

With love, Dud

This letter followed in the packet.

June 20, 1910
Dudley S. Conley, M.D.
342 West 56th Street, New York

My Dearest Sweetheart—

I can't tell you how much I thank you for the good things you sent me nor far more for the dandy letter you write. Don't mind, Bess, if I do not answer but just think, dear, such is the nature of the brute and remember that I love you more and more all the time. From the way things look, Bess, I think it will not be so very long before we can marry and then—well I think I shall not have loved quietly in vain for I shall have the dandiest wife imaginable. I wonder, girl, if you love me as much as I care for you? Perhaps not but what is the difference, maybe you will someday.

I have just been appointed Instructor in College of Physicians and Surgeons, to demonstrate bedside surgery to the students who come down to Belleview. Quite an honor but wholly undeserved for I am a regular "mutt" so far as I am concerned. But in giving me the place the powers who be assured me it would lead to something better. Since it only pays $50.00 a month I hope so. How I wish you were with me, Bess, for I believe success would be much easier with you by my side. Now write to me, dearest, and don't mind if I don't answer for you must know that I am yours, heart, body, & soul.

With Love, Dud

Having no responses from Bess and no evidence in her journaling of this friendship, we can only assume that this couple was not meant to be. The romance may have been rather one-sided between two ambitious professionals whose paths crossed while she was working at Bellevue and he was working as a resident and instructor of surgery at Columbia.

The State Historical Society of Missouri contains correspondence, diaries, scrapbooks, accounts, and miscellaneous items of the Conleys, a prominent Boone County family. In the biographical sketches of family members is the following paragraph about Dudley S. Conley, MD: *"Dudley Steele Conley, surgeon and dean of the University of Missouri School of Medicine, was born in Columbia, Missouri, 26 January 1878. He received a B.L., University of Missouri, 1899, and an M.D. from Columbia University, New York, 1905. He married Sidney A. Boales on 2 January 1915. While practicing surgery in New York, 1909–1918, he also served as an instructor in surgery at Columbia, 1912–1918, and attended postgraduate medical school, 1916–1918. He was a professor of surgery, University of Missouri School of Medicine, 1919–1933; and was appointed dean in 1933. He served in the U.S. Army Medical Reserve Medical Corps, 1917–1919. Memberships included the American College of Surgeons, American Medical Association, and Missouri State Medical Association, vice president, 1935, and president, 1937.'*

Looking closer to home after the family crises ended, Bess accepted a position with the Denver Visiting Nurse Association. Her training and experience qualified her for superintendent and executive director of the program. One of her favorite projects during her two years with Denver VNA was her initiation of the infant welfare stations in neighborhoods that provided maternal-child health care for mothers and babies. Her staff of visiting nurses provided this care and promoted educational programs for their patients. During her "watch" she changed the uniform hat from a long flowing veil to a more practical smart sailor hat with a brim. Her concern was always to make working conditions better and improve asepsis in health care given. These changes assisted the nurse in comfort and in her care. Bess was also instrumental in encouraging and implementing improved educational and service standards for professional public-health nurses.

More background is found in the "75th Anniversary History of Denver VNA": "It became increasingly obvious to all of the visiting nurse associations of the United States that a national organization was needed in order to improve educational and service standards and to promote acceptance of the work of the public health nurse. The Denver Visiting Nurse Association was active in this movement from its onset, and was one of the early organizations to join the newly organized National Organization of Public Health Nurses." Bess was an active member of this organization.

The autumn 1965 issue of the Denver VNA newsletter noted that a VNA career runs in the family as Alice Stephenson, RN, was a Denver VNA staff nurse at that time. It had an article to add to this history: "*Her [Alice's] aptitude for and interest in public health nursing has a natural stimulus in the career of her aunt, Elizabeth Shellabarger. Elizabeth Shellabarger was Superintendent of the Visiting Nurse Association from 1910 to 1912, when the staff consisted of one obstetrical nurse, two staff nurses, and one other employee. One major item under her jurisdiction was the establishment of the first well -baby clinic. One minor one, but of interest, is that it was Miss Shellabarger who discarded the big flowing hat as part of the VNA uniform and replaced it with something more trim and practical. At the age of 70 Miss Shellabarger is still taking specialized training at the University of Arizona and continues to teach and give occasional lectures.*"

Bess enjoyed her time in Denver during her VNA years and was active in the Episcopal Church, American Red Cross, and several book and study groups that filled her after-work hours.

Several pamphlets in the suitcases of memorabilia contained information about the VNA years. One listed past superintendents and executive directors of Denver VNA from 1889 at its founding to 1955. Miss E. Shellabarger is listed with the year 1910.

Another article discussed the progress of Denver Visiting Nurse Association. Bess wrote *"1911"* on the margin of one stating the following: *"The Denver Visiting Nurse Association has been placed in charge of the Day Camp recently opened at the Bryant School in Denver by the 'Daily News'. The camp is supported by public subscription. It is hoped that it will pave the way for a larger Infant Welfare Society late. Elizabeth Shellabarger, Bellevue Hospital, New York, is the Superintendent of Nurses of the Denver Visiting Nurse Association. Marie Arbisher, Illinois Training School, Chicago has been the visiting tuberculosis nurse for the association since last December."*

A caption included with the following photo stated interesting information about the VNA of the time. It states as follows: *"1910— 1919 It became increasingly obvious to all of the visiting nurse associations of the United States that a national organization was needed in order to improve educational and service standards and to promote acceptance of the work of the public health nurse. The Denver Visiting Nurse Association was active in this movement from its onset, and was one of the early organizations to join the newly organized National Organization of Public Health Nursing. In 1912, a very important aspect of service was implemented, the Infant Welfare Stations. Another program directed to the health of children was started. This was supervision of public playgrounds. In 1917, the United States entered World War I, and a shortage of nursing personnel for civilian purposes resulted. In 1918, the year of the great influenza epidemic, the work of the staff tripled despite the fact that no new positions were added.'*

Bess became actively involved in the development of the National Organization of Public Health Nurses and was a lifelong member. She felt the organization of professional nurses and creation of a network of nurses with a common focus were paramount in the quality, continuing education and support of her peers. She wrote many letters, articles, and talks for this organization and for the American Nurses Association and Colorado, Texas, Utah, and Arkansas Nurses Associations as they matured.

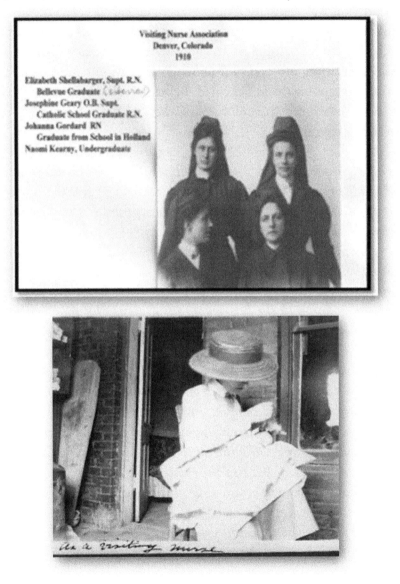

Visiting Nurse Association
Denver, Colorado
1910

Elizabeth Shellabarger, Supt. R.N.
  Bellevue Graduate (deceased)
Josephine Geary O.B. Supt.
  Catholic School Graduate R.N.
Johanna Gordard RN
  Graduate from School in Holland
Naomi Kearny, Undergraduate

As a visiting nurse

Bess received a letter, in 1912, from an administrator in Salt Lake City with whom she had established a connection in one of her nursing organizations. She was offered a job instructing in a new program of nursing education. She felt she had left her mark on the Denver VNA programs and was ready for a new challenge. She accepted the job offer. From 1912 to 1916 as superintendent of the school of nursing at Saint Mark's Hospital in Salt Lake City, her tireless enthusiasm for improving nursing education and constant networking with nursing organizations and nursing schools made Bess glad she had accepted this open position that she loved. From the Saint Mark's School of Nursing website, we learn the following:

Finding trained nurses was also difficult for St. Mark's. The need for trained nurses became critical with the new 35 bed facility, and it was almost impossible to encourage nurses from Eastern schools to come to Utah.

Taking the problem into its own hands, the St. Mark's Hospital School of Nursing was founded in 1894, just 21 years after the first nurse had graduated in the United States. This was the first training school for nurses in the Intermountain Region. This tradition continues today at the St. Mark's Hospital/Westminster College School of Nursing. The first superintendent of the school was Miss Mary Edith Newitt. She arrived on February 12, 1894, and promptly told the administration that conditions were "abominable." Soon afterward, standards changed. Instruments were sterilized in the basement kitchen and carried upstairs in hot pans. Large quantities of carbolic acid and bichloride were used as disinfectants. Surgeons did not wear masks, but tied their hair back.

Cotton gloves were occasionally used on septic patients, however, in most cases gloves were not used. In 1895, St. Mark's replaced a rickety express wagon and cot with a new horse-drawn ambulance service. Hospital Superintendent D. Douglas Wallace, proudly reported to the Board of Directors, *"Our ambulance, which is the only one in the city, has been invaluable and a great boon to those unfortunate enough to meet with accidents."* One hundred years later, Wallace would be proud, if not a little amazed, by St. Mark's Hospital's ability to transport patients via helicopter. In 1908, a typhoid epidemic pushed St. Mark's Hospital beyond the breaking point. Emergency tents had to be sent up to handle the additional patients. In the late 1800s and early 1900s, typhoid with the third most common disease treated at the hospital. The nurses, though well-trained at the St. Mark's Hospital School of Nursing, were not immune. Miss Beatrice Smith, class of 1899, wrote, *"Several nurses were victims of typhoid fever, and two students died".* During the first week I was in training one died and it cast a gloom over the whole hospital. The other was in my class and died about a year later.

Years later family members would draw to mind the history of Bess at Saint Mark's, when her eldest grandnephew, Ralph Porter Selch, was born at Saint Mark's Hospital in 1929 and when her great-grandnephew, Brian Charles Stephenson, was born in this same hospital in 1970. In May of 2013, her great-great-grandniece, Leah Michele Jeglum, granddaughter of Dorothy Selch Jeglum, would graduate from Saint Mark's School of Nursing with her BSN degree. The amazing legacy continued.

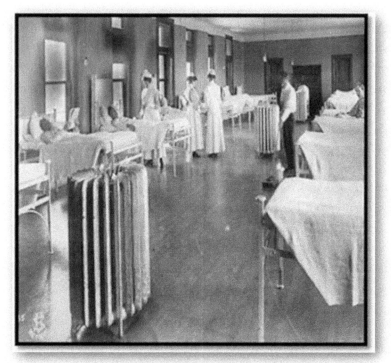

Bess (third from left) supervising students at
Saint Mark's Hospital in Salt Lake City, Utah.

The death of Adam Shellabarger in 1916 again brought Bess home to the San Luis Valley for six months. Her expertise and skills were helpful to family members and especially her mother as they adjusted to life without the patriarch. When life returned to some normalcy at the ranch, she again went to the Denver area to seek work. This time she worked in Boulder, Colorado, in initiating their visiting-nurse service. It was from this experience that she decided that, in order to fill the positions that excited her most and to fulfill her continued thirst for learning, she must return to school for her BS degree.

Bess applied at Columbia University in New York City, and off she went across the country again to school. Some of her credits from Emerson College were accepted toward her degree, and she pursued a course of study that would assist her in fields of public health, instruction of nurses, and teaching health and hygiene. At that time, the majority of professional nurses were graduates of three-year programs with a focus primarily on clinical skills with little instruction in basic sciences, nutrition, asepsis, or critical thinking. All of these issues were of vital interest to Bess. Pursuing this degree would have a major impact on the skills she took forward into her career. She launched into her planned studies for the autumn of 1916 and the spring and summer of 1917. Her sister Eloise was also working in New York City. The diary pages told of her experiences:

Sept. 30, 1916: 1st Chem class arranged for classes in Harlem.

Oct. 1, 1916: To Bronx Park. Could not find Eloise who came for me at Harlem at 3 p.m. Went to St. John's the Divine at 4 p.m.

Oct. 2nd: 9 a.m. to Dr. Cook's office for asthma treatment. Class all rest of the day,

Oct. 3rd: Shopped on way to college before 10 a.m. Studied all day until after midnight. Bought swimming suit for 50 cents.

Oct. 6th: Nursing and Health class in room 2077. Eloise came to see me after dinner.

Oct. 9th: Studied all a.m. then had lunch at Harlem before first Psychology class at 1 p.m.

Oct. 12th: Good spirit at Teacher's College. Quite Democratic. Psychology teacher says Columbia is opposed to lecture system.

Oct. 18th: Just one year ago at 10:00 today dear Father was taken from us, Oh! Such a terrible year without him.

Oct. 19th: Rained so hard could not go to Alumna meeting at Bellevue & get back in time for class. Did not call Eloise today.

Oct. 28th: A letter from Walter in New Mexico & Blanche also, saying children all have whooping cough. Dr. Wall again called for the evening and took Eloise and me to dinner.

December 2, 1916: Studied Chem all a.m. then went to Atlantic Fleet with Eloise in p.m. and to see President Wilson light the statue of Liberty.

January 7, 1917: Very wicked, stayed home and worked on paper for tomorrow all day.

January 8th: Dr. Gano was waiting for me as I came home at 6 p.m. and took me to the Hippodrome, then to supper. Received birthday cake for Eloise from Mother

January 14th. Went to Hotel Lafayette to dinner with Miss Lenhart from Bellevue. To Grace Church first then had Birthday Party for Eloise with three guests.

January 17th: Heard from letters about Walter and Mae leaving New Mexico. Bellevue Alumni meeting. Eloise and I are taking swim lessons. I am learning to swim on my side. Finished signing Father's estate

February 28, 1917: Walter has bought the Friars Ranch. Went to dinner with Eloise at Waldorf Astoria.

DISASTER STRUCK!!! THE BEGINNING OF WORLD WAR I.

Bess on Jim before leaving for the war.

FORM NO. 6

BUREAU OF NURSING SERVICE
WASHINGTON, D. C.

JANE A. DELANO

Miss M. Elizabeth Shellabarger,
2?? Bellaire St,
Denver, Col.

Dear Madam:

Enclosed you will find your appointment card and badge, the numbers on which correspond. No. 7???

Will you please acknowledge the receipt of same on the enclosed postal card and for verification kindly give number?

Since secretaries of local committees notify nurses called for active service, it is important that correct names and addresses be filed with them. Nurses failing to report change of address may be dropped from enrollment list, as provided in our rules.

Assuring you of our appreciation of your enrollment, believe me,

Sincerely yours,

Jane A. Delano

Chairman National Committee,
Red Cross Nursing Service.

1917. Bess (third from right) in Red Cross uniform.

The War Year

*A*t the beginning of the war, Bess felt compelled to do more than complete school. Coming back home with her degree unfinished in the fall of 1917, she joined the University of Colorado Hospital Unit—which became a Red Cross nursing unit for World War I duty. While waiting to be called up, she worked as superintendent of a private hospital in Cheyenne, Wyoming. Bess joined the Army Nurse Reserve Corps and was sent to Fort Riley, Kansas. She did American Red Cross duty until the nurses were sent to New York City and then served overseas as assistant chief nurse in London and Winchester, England, until appointed chief nurse of the hospital ship *Saxonia*. The following letter describes being called up:

February 19, 1918 Denver, COLORADO Called by Chief Beecroft RN on phone that 10 nurses had been called to report at Ft. Riley and I had been put in charge & ordered to buy tickets. Signed oath at 2 p.m. under Wm. Spaulding & left in mail box. Bought 8 tickets at U.P. Office & promptly stopped to get Liberty Bond Certificate at U.S. Nat. Bank. Have no time to get receipt from safety box at Colo. Nat. Could not receive Bond—left until after the war. Hurried to Eva's to pack. Met nurses with checks at depot 6 p.m. & listed baggage. Mother met me there. Had dinner at Oxford Hotel. Nurses met at 8:20 to leave on U.P. Train but did not leave for two hrs. Saw "Extra Denver Times with all names in the first column. (Mother & Mr. I Sutton stayed to see us off.). Have 5 uppers and 4 lowers in Pullman. Breakfast at 9:30 a.m., took Kodak pictures at Salina, Kan. Arrived Ft. Riley 2:30 p.m.

Feb. 20. Met by Ambulance U.S.. To Chief nurses office for expense account. To Community Room—COLD, VERY COLD. No rooms for nurses left at Ft. Riley. Assigned to sleep on porches, awfully cold. Later room for one. 9:00a.m.

February 21, 1918 I went on duty, Specialized Ward. Met Lt. Col Williams from home.

Feb. 22, 1918 Vaccinated 2 p.m..

February 23, 1918 Miss. Benson Brain RN (from St. Marks in Salt Lake) met at dinner. 5p.m. got more in expense account from Denver. Assigned to hospital to start duty.

March 4th: Brother Rafe's birthday. Had a tedious time in the ward today waiting for Dr. Lt. Enberg who came back twice to do dressings. Lt. Dr. Gather finished his dressings quickly. Went out to the trenches after duty with a lovely southern girl, Miss Robertson, and Mrs. K. who was a special nurse at our ranch for Mr. Benton once upon a time & knows Rafe and Walter. She is a graduate from Miss Converses' School in Wyoming.

The trenches look like play houses, latticed walls of willows. Latrines built with square oil can retainers. Heating systems BAD, too hot in and too cold outside. In our ward of 35 patients nearly all are getting well. Erysipelas case now in side room but another case developing a swollen ear. Trying to institute the sterilizing of instruments between cases by boiling, but ward surgeon thinks alcohol is sufficient. Went to first French class tonight which was held in mess hall. Wore Emma's old blue taffeta dress today with great comfort. French teacher will come daily. (we'll meet in my room next time and be cooler).   She, Miss Mordell, was born in Germany and educated in France, came to U.S. on the "Vaterland" which never returned but was taken by the U.S. when war was declared.

Erysipelas is a skin infection, similar to cellulites, that is caused by the bacteria streptococcus. Prior to antibiotics, there was little but symptomatic treatment, and it was very contagious. Bess had an innate ability to see the benefit of sterilization and hand washing as a preventive of these easily transferable diseases. Multiple times in her diaries, she told of trying to suggest and implement boiling, hand washing, and isolation to prevent spread of infections.

March 9th: Kansas wind is almost a cyclone today as I walk across the parade grounds to my station. More recruits coming in—a company of Indians and Mexicans are in quarters. T.B. ward is full. Some patients drafted from T.B. Sanitariums or cases not recognized by local Physicians. Three nurses are sick.

March 11th: First day to be tired out. Did half the dressings alone when Capt. was called to OR. Patient, Ralph Lyon, is going to leave Thursday to drive his ambulance through to the coast, then off to France. (A handsome fellow). He says he WILL be a Lieutenant before it is over. Patient Eaton said some of the nurses make the corners of the beds look so well "they are just like rose buds". A good honest boy, grateful for kindnesses. Patient Geary said before nurses came temperatures were never taken until patients dropped.

March 12th: Patient died who was taken from ward with Meningitis. Had military funeral today. Our Denver Nurse, Miss Roach is worse

March 13th: *32 nurses ill—throats, ears, and grippe. I did the dressings mostly alone today. We have a dietitian in charge of mess hall now and our service is better.*

March 14th: *Had Schick Test today, a little antitoxin to see if we are susceptible to Diphtheria. Given the Caduceus emblem for our collars today—brass but just like the Army Nurses.*

March 27th: *Caps and Red Cross Capes issued today. I'm almost sick with a cold and getting a bad cough. Had positive reaction to Schick test for diphtheria. Dr. said I should not be put on contagious ward and if necessary be given antitoxin. I should be sanitized first because of hay-fever & danger of anaphylaxis. One of our Denver Nurses has mumps and another just getting well.*

March 28ᵗʰ: *A rumor going around that germs have been found in the OP room sterilizer—placed there by some Pro-German Dr. or Nurse—which may be responsible for the infected mastoid cases. I personally think it is the absence of surgical technique by such Drs. as one on our ward that has caused all the trouble. I wonder if such dreadful M.D.'s are Pro-German and try to kill of our men here or are they just ignorant of modern methods.*

April 16th: *Cases transferred from the ward with diphtheria and some as diphtheria carriers. Meningitis patient died. The other CU Unit Nurses were all transferred to a camp in Illinois.*

May 2nd: *I was made charge nurse in Ward L-65, where I have been on night duty.*

May 11th: *Dr. Raines (well liked Dr.) admitted with 104 degree temp. Fear meningitis. He is so well liked.*

May 12th: Lt. Raines better today. Fever caused by a protein formed from the Dakin's Solution used in dressing wounds. Doctors say some people are susceptible, like an anaphylaxis.

May 16th: Went to Kansas Nurses Association meeting to talk about contaminants. (given the day off to do this). Working nights, sometimes 12 hr. duty, and often only getting 6 hrs. sleep during the day. It felt good to do something normal during the day. Awfully tired.

May 19th: Went to YWCA Hostess House. A Crowd of mothers, wives, and sisters were trying to find their soldiers. What would they do without the Hostess House.

The following article, headlined "Miss Mary Elizabeth Shellabarger Ministers to Soldiers at Funston," was posted in the *Saguache Crescent* with a picture of Bess:

MARY ELIZABETH SHELLABARGER.

Miss Mary Elizabeth Shellabarger of 2810 Bellaire street, daughter of Mrs. Adam Shellabarger of Moffat, Colo., is at Fort Riley, ministering to the needs of sick soldiers at Camp Funston, while awaiting orders to go "over there" with base hospital No. 29.

Miss Shellabarger is one of the most enthusiastic helpers of the Y. W. C. A. at their hostess house, which is the gathering place of Camp Funston. When not on active duty at the camp hospital Miss Shellabarger is busy bringing mother and son together, locating husbands for young wives, who naturally gravitate to the hostess house when arriving in the camp, since the corps of women who comprise the camp workers at the Y. W. C. A. know just how to locate any one in the camp.

So busy has the young nurse been and so absorbed in the many activities in which the Y. W. C. A. engages at the camp to make life as enjoyable as possible for the soldier whose time hangs heavy on his hands, that she presented the hostess house with a goodly check to be used in their work.

Her friends here are delighted with the reports she sends them. She has not regretted her decision to go to France—on the contrary, she expresses impatience at the delay.

May 23rd: It is thought that the awful Meningitis Epidemic of last fall was caused by inoculation by German spy M.D.'s at Funston. Rumor says some are serving at Leavenworth now who were caught. Went horseback riding with Miss Ruff at 11a.m.—perfectly glorious with so many flowers and our horses were good. Like riding through a real garden, spider wort, yellow dock, moss roses and wild roses.

May 26th: Orders to report to New York are here. I got weak in the knees at the thought of dear mother.

May 28th: Telegram from Mother this a.m. How I hate to leave the dears at home. I know now why Father was taken from us, as this would be so hard for him, but Mother understands.

May 29th: Relieved of duty, said goodbye to patients and had lass class for corpsmen at 4p.m. Packed and sent box home. Got transportation from quartermaster and went ahead to reserve Pullman. 34 cents for all of us.

May 30, 1918: DECORATION DAY: Left Ft. Riley Kansas on way to Europe via New York City. (learned to knit enroute to New York) Wish to be at Rito Alto Cemetery with home people today but start at 12:10pm for New York via Union Pacific to Kansas City & Sante Fe R.R. to Chicago then New York Central to New York City. Expect to get in Sat. night so I wired Eloise (who is in N.Y.) to look for us. (11 Nurses)

June 1st–11th: New York City. Stayed in three different hotels and had to answer roll call at 10a.m. daily. Saw the sights and visited with Eloise until she left for home June 9th. Anxious to get going and join our unit overseas.

June 15th: Went with the whole unit to Hoboken to have finger prints taken and have photographs taken. Returned by 24rd St. ferry. Saw "Vaterland" and many boats loaded to the brim with soldiers. All boats camouflaged. Took some nurses down to Columbia then down through Bellevue. I'm proud of graduating from there.

June 25th: They are to give us list of their donations to us. Fitted for gray uniforms and rain coats. Went to Red Cross Headquarters at 9 a.m. where Miss Johnson R.N. talked to our unit. Then to 222 4th Ave for Red Cross

July 2nd: Chaplain Hollaway talked to the nurses at Roll Call while I was excused to make rounds in the nurse's rooms with two soldiers to mark the trunks and suit cases. Signed our wills before Lawyer with a witness there. Going to send one copy for my safety box and the other to Eloise to keep.

July 4th: 8 a.m. Met with the Unit in front of the Greenwich Theater to march in the parade. Marched from Washington Square up 5th Ave. to 72nd St. in white uniforms and Red Cross Capes. A few units in the blue overseas uniforms. Bought a jersey utility dress at Franklins for $18.50 after looking all over for a dress to wear on the boat. The silk poplin of the Red Cross uniform is rather too elaborate to sleep in through the danger zone. Received our life saving suits. Fitted them on and went to drill tired out.

July 8th: Signed for 2 hats, blue serge uniform, 4 gray uniforms and blanket steamer roll sleeping bag and underwear. Miss Martha Russell RN came to look on and Miss Johnson RN was there in the assemblage in the dining room of Arlington Hotel. My things all fit, thankfully. Every nurse was given a pink rose when the uniforms were distributed.

July 10th: My Blanket roll was packed by a soldier yesterday, but left no room --he packed an Army blanket, sleeping bag, my extra red and green blanket, rubber boots, 2 pr. shoes, rain coat & hat, bath robe & two sweaters. I opened it later & put in soap, cold cream, and little extra with 2 hanks of gray wool.

The nurses and troops embarked on the *Olympic* for Tottenham, London, duty until after Armistice Day.

July 12th: 9 a.m. after breakfast all hands ordered by bugle on deck. Nurses on top, troops on lower decks, to stand at attention with white life belts on for instructions from the British Embarkation Officer. 9:10 steamed out from New York Dock (A clever plan to have all passengers accounted for!!). Ordered to wear the chest life belts until further notice. The troops wearing black ones and we and the officers have white canvas ones. Stood in line most the day getting safety suits. A.U Boats destroyer preceded us all day.

During transit, played cards, knit, and attended lectures and church services. Read & play cards when rainy, and walk deck for exercise daily. Half the girls sea sick with rough water, but I am fine. Nearly froze during the night as we passed an iceberg. Some nurses on duty with pneumonia cases. Meals are fair but desserts are queer. Rice and prunes served on large serving platters.

July 19th: Shore in sight, docked in the evening, much yelling and shouting.

July 20th: The boys are singing as they march off the boat. It makes me feel like weeping to see them. Many rumors as to our destination. Reached NorthEastern Hospital about 5:30 p.m. Served in Awaiting more orders. Toured Buckingham Palace, Tower of London, a Cinema, Royal Botanical Gardens, Bedford School for

*Women & London University. Went shopping for an umbrella—
store right out of Dickens!! Wandered lovely English Lanes and had
dinner at a farmhouse of tea & waffles. Raining much of the time
& very cold. Saw the King Knight 2 old men.*

*July 26th: At home all day very uncomfortable in the cold. Rained
several times. Many air ships went over the hospital. Search lights in
the sky all evening.*

*August 4th: News from U.S. through YMCA makes me think Walter,
Rafe, & Nick may be included soon. British Transport sunk crossing
the Channel with Australian wounded—nearly 200 in Hospital
Ship lost. Started our work in the hospital wards with the wounded.*

*August 6th: Went on night duty as first night nurse until I'm night
Chief. Had five sick corpsmen all from Colorado. Thankful for an
American Nurse, our patient said the bed spread made him think of
salt cellar, tooth pick holders & strong smell in the cupboard.*

*August 10th: First night as Night Chief. Three supper shifts during
the night in the Kitchen. Two tables full of nurses following a table
of Corpsmen. Three cooks are fairly good, they start making biscuits
for 500 at 3 a.m.*

*August 12th. Rainy only half the day. Not at all sleepy all night
since had such an undisturbed day. Two more nurses on duty. Wards
opened E and #37. The soldiers are simply tickled to death to get
here where they can be cared for by Americans. Poor boys have seen
all and suffered all that is horrible. Find that Private Moore is in
our unit on porch. A Colo man with M.A. from Boulder University
and is much more interesting than many of higher rank. Has a good
sound philosophy of life. Interviewed by a Salt Lake Newspaper
reporter.*

August 21st: Ten wards are open now. Patients come in fast by convoy—arriving mostly at night, 75–200 at a time.

August 26th: Had a hard night. Many admissions. Patients had been so transferred about to make possible the painting of wards. Last night for the eight a.m. shifts had forty nurses at midnight supper at two tables in the big kitchen. Admitted 89 patients. Ran into some Colorado soldiers and Doctors and several Doctors from Bellevue. Patients coming from France (7 hours away) very badly wounded. All hungry and glad to have the supper served as they came in at 9 p.m. and 3 a.m. Receiving mail from home about a month from its mailing date. Everything is censored.

August 27th. Raining and cold. I had sixteen nurses on duty last night for 12 hours. Our pt. in #10 did not return all night (worried). Capt. Kirkham was O.D., seems just as business like and capable as he is handsome. It takes me three hours in evening to make complete rounds and 2 hours in a.m. The search lights were many last evening and different from the usual. Birds (aeroplanes) were flying early this a.m.

August 28th. The poor boys admitted tonight had awful fractures and amputations.

August 30th. Kept my Sargent Keeley on the jump delivering notes to the Med Officers about patients tonight and changing duties for corpsmen. No letters today, we are all terribly disappointed.

September 1st. 18 night nurses on duty, another ward opened #35 for general surgical. The Col. is not taking names as the boys come over the fence. Much chafing under army discipline amongst the nurses as well as the men. After an hour of sleep main called me at 9:30 a.m. for church and then Chaplain Yates did not hold service in our little Chapel. I don't like him anyhow. 11 a.m. Service in Y.M tent under my window kept me awake but I'm glad some one had pep enough for a service.

Sept. 3rd. Wonderful lights in the sky tonight, counted over forty. Wish I could write home about them. Found a Dr. (Lt) White from Bellevue in D, a melancholia case, he is cousin of our Lily White of Old Bellevue, he knew Eddie Armstrong and Dud Conley. A letter from Mother dated Rito Alto Aug 4. I wept for joy over it and a wonderful letter from Walter and one from Dollie and a postal from Eloise. Wrote a letter to Rafe. Tonight twenty three new patients straight from France in tonight very badly wounded.

September 9th. A wonderful day, slept from 9:30 to 7. Too bad to have to rush on duty without supper—but how good I feel after my hard, busy time with many sick patients last night. We expected 50 patients tonight and admitted only 15 after nurses worked like mad to prepare a new ward. Sgt Keeley has worked so well he has quite redeemed himself in the eyes of his men who knew he had fought his sargentry, he will do anything for me so I keep him busy considering he has never before worked.

September 10th: Occasionally have a good sleeping day, but usually only about 6 hours. I have been freezing, but had had no fire—the Colonel ordered us to conserve fuel by burning no fuel for comfort. All grate fires in our quarters must be stopped and only fires in the ward kitchens are allowed. Dreadfully cold and we are layering everything we own to keep warm.

September 11th. The Chief Army Nurse, Miss Leonard told our Dietitian today we are not getting even the English Army rations and she must give us more food. Consequently we had steak for supper. I like our plain food with no dessert. I've had not one stomach spell since coming to London. I try to be a good fellow and drink tea with Miss Hurst in the a.m. but it is too strong and I do not like it at 5:30 a.m.

September 16th. The English Ivy is wonderfully green all wet and shiny. The fig trees in front of Ward 19 are pretty, the old-fashioned garden at contageous ward is lovely and a beautiful geranium and a queer lavendar flower grow. Spiderwort is cultivated in the London yards. Search lights are not so many and bright. Sketched Elder Berries and Horse Chestnuts from window before going to bed. The nurses (3) we admitted from France seem inclined to criticise our appointments, they should be very grateful to come to this good place. They say they didn't like the care in a Brit Hospital with English M.D.'s and Sisters.

September 24th: Last night we admitted two wards full of influenza cases from the States, so terribly sick. The first time I've done enough work to make my circulation actually start since coming to London. Interviewed Colonel Anderson this a.m. on Infectious Precautions, and before night had orders for masks to be worn by all nurses and attendants in the influenza wards. Those terribly sick boys first landed from America on the same steamer we came on, so many weeks ago. I hope the whole Hospital will not get Influenza from the lax precautions in isolation of the cases.

September 30th. Only one death the night shift. Holmes, the first soldier we expected to pass away had T.B. The Pneumonia influenza ward is a different place since Capt Huardstrom took charge, his is a well trained man. Windows were all opened, wire masks provided for attendants and all attendants ordered to get into fresh air five minutes every 3 hours. Gave opiate for pain or stir *only when awake. We may save some of these cases now from the "Olympic".*

October 1st: I went to bed and shivered all day with sore throat. The nurses from France though all sick somehow seem to stand this cold better than our unit. Looks as if the war will not last long since Bulgaria has made unconditional surrender to Allies.

October 3rd: Walked miles last night to cover ground after 127 patients were admitted. So many sick nurses, too. We have two new M.D.'s from the British Forces in France. A letter came from Mabel saying that Lou is now a Major and that Henry has been in France over a year. His hair has turned white and he is very tired. Mabel has been ill. During the night Miss Orgren was so terribly low, I called her best friend at 3 a.m. to sit with her. It does not seem possible we might lose her. So many nurses sick with Spanish Influenza we hardly have enough to keep the wards going. My voice is gone, but I can now stay with my work because the chills and fever I had the first of the week have disappeared. I can't keep my vow to myself to go to bed when ill—there are too many off at present.

October 4th: Just as I came on duty at 6:45 p.m. Miss Orgren died in Ward E, the first to go from our nursing staff. There was a beautiful tradition of caring for he. The body of our "Beautiful Angel of Mercy" was taken to the morgue this morning and I accompanied it to the door. At evening the body was prepared and placed in beautiful repose on the couch in upper reception room, dressed in white uniform and Red Cross Cap covered with the protective U.S. Flag and with her head resting on the Red Cross Flag, the symbol of comfort. The R.C. Nurses wreath of white chrysanthemums at the head and Red Cross Laurel leaf wreath at foot. Pink roses from army nurse organization and others on the table at sides and orchid with oak leaves and roses from nurses of 29, and violets from St. Lukes Nurses. She will be given Military burial. Her body was later placed in a plain pine casket without handles and with flag draped over top and carried by two Corpsmen from Nurses reception Room to the hearse which was driven to station at 7:30 p.m. She will have a military burial.

October 9th. Corpsmen of Unit 29 were put into tents today, they are pretty cross about it because there are no proper platform floors. The boards are placed right on the ground and this ground is wet. The men would not object if the officers and non coms took pot luck with them as in France, but they all have the rest rooms available.

The Corpsmen had their first dance in mess hall tonight and had nice English girls out here. One who came in to phone for her Father to meet her at the tube terminal was a lovely little lady. Another of our poor boys from the Olympic died tonight.

October 15th: Clear and warmer. Came on duty to be greeted at 8:05 with the death of Clifford Hellis, our best corpsman from Ward 31. Two more or three have pneumonia—thirty five men have influenza or pneumonia since they have been placed in tents on this wet ground awaiting the finish of their quarters which will never be ready—these slow English workmen. All this time one big bldg stands empty. Another death at 2:30 a.m., a Lieut. Walker of Flying Corps. Another death from pneumonia at 3 a.m. an Engl. workman. The patient with pneumonia is not treated in the army but the disease is treated from Washington with statistics here and in the camps.

October 16th: My Birthday: I have barely been getting around. I know I have the flu, but just keep going. We have trouble keeping the delirious boys in bed. They think this is their dorm. Losing corpsmen and 16 nurses ill from Influenza and Pneumonia (Plague).

October 21st: *We are almost overwhelmed with the influenza plague which is spreading over London, over the whole World, in fact. There are no vaccines in London to immunize the command, as is the custom in infected districts of the U.S.A. I've decided to do something to save my sanity, I am taking organ lessons from the organist at St. Anne's Church. The organ is one played by Mendelssohn.*

October 25th. *Three more nurses have died in Edmunton Hospital from Influenza. Two nursing journals arrived by post with no postage. The bill must have passed for sending periodicals to Ex Forces without charge. Another delirium case lost his head tonight. I think these shell shock cases are more cigarette and whiskey d than shell insanity just as the men and officers in the Philippines went insane from dissipation. Lt. Pritchard an example.*

October 31st. *Relieved from night duty. Up at 3 p.m. and went down to Postmaster Row where I bought two beautiful tiny prayer books and some Xmas cards. A Halloween party was given in the house tonight. We dressed up as old ladies.*

Nov. 1st. *Clear day. Took charge of Wd 32—had only one nurse to help me. Miss Richmond is not so good as Miss Gjellum who was on sick report. After a wild day in the ward I went to St. Annes and practiced my organ lesson. David Phillips the nice Eng. boy did the blowing. Miss Rathel is desperately sick tonight. This is the 20th day of her pneumonia. She knew me and talked this afternoon, poor girl. I am so sorry for her, has had a hard life since her mother deserted her family.*

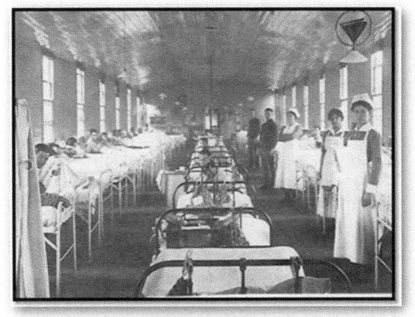

Ward 32 World War I

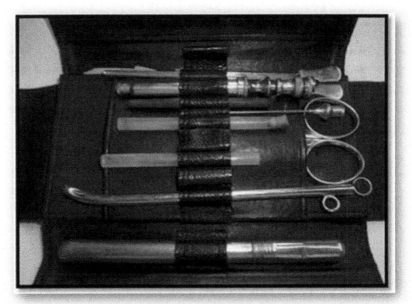

Pocket medical kit carried by World War I nurses.
Vials contained morphine and quinine.

November 7th: PEACE!! Strong rumors that the war is ended to-night. The men in the ward are all happy and talking like old veterans. Have worked like lightening from 7 a.m. until 10:30 p.m. today only stopping to eat. Fortunately the harder we work the better we are fed. Our chief trouble still is the good for nothing corpsmen we brought from Denver who came into the medical Corps for "safety" and now are too good for their work at the time and are dodging work. London is now a busy place with over 1100 patients. Another Colorado Nurse came to my ward today and we really did some nursing and finished without neglecting the poor boys.

Bess then was sent to rest camp number thirty-five in Winchester, England, as assistant chief nurse. Her final tour was on the *Transport Saxonia*, where she served as chief nurse to sail from Gravesend, England, with 1,400 sick and war-injured boys. They landed in New York City after Christmas 1918.

November 11th: "THE ARMISTICE" The Armistice was signed today at 11:a.m. and the city went wild. Walks are crowded and flags flying from every window. Green Lanes near Salisbury Corner, the buses and tube were so crowded that everyone was late in getting home from London.

November 18th: Received orders for change of duty to Winchester. Packed up and went by Ambulance and train. Given charge of three flu wards. Very cold and wet. Colored patients from Alabama are freezing.

December 3rd: Received orders to return to America. I as Chief in Charge of 14 Nurses. Sent out half of the patients to Hersley in a big van. All happy to go even those on crutches.

<u>December 12th</u>: *Took the train to London in charge of 12 nurses to board "Saxonia" at Gravesend. Met at Liverpool Street Station where we were met by Miss Porter and 15 more nurses for me to take charge of on duty for the voyage. Got on the ship before the patients so unpacked all goods and supplies. Loaded patients all the next day and I assigned my nurses—a hard job when not acquainted with the work of the nurses from other units. Some of them have bad habits—smoking and loitering. Loaded more patients the next day, swinging them up from the wharf in a wooden box with four men standing on the platform. I have a stateroom for office and bedroom.*

<u>December 14, 1918</u>: *Sailed at 6p.m. Wonderful waves and storm at sea. Many sea-sick, but I revel in the grandeur. A few more nurses on duty and all patients doing well. The dressings and care of compound fractures take much time. The Red Cross gave all of the men a box of candy today. They are giving out something special each day—Champagne, Port wine, a Medical supply box, a canteen, and music on ship.*

<u>Christmas Day at Sea</u>: *Foggy half the day but had a sumptuous breakfast, a chicken lunch, and a wonderful plum pudding dinner but the turkey was poorly cooked. We also had "Well Done America" cake. We had a party last night on deck with singing, a program, and dancing*

<u>December 26th</u>: *Met by the Atlantic Fleet as we steamed in the Hudson River. Met with blowing whistles, ringing bells, and a band on the dock. Red Cross workers began unloading patients after lunch and I sent 19 nurses to Polyclinic Hospital at 7P.M., just retaining enough nurses for night duty. Smuggled Eloise to the boat for a visit.*

A *New York Times* article titled "*1400 Wounded Reach Gotham*" states, "*New York, Dec. 26—Following the homecoming battle fleet into port came the British liner 'Saxonia' from Liverpool with 1,400 sick and wounded officers and men, mostly surgical cases."*

Bess aboard SS Saxonia

It is like living again to breathe this clear air, but our skin feels dry after so much rain of England. Last patient left the ship on a stretcher at noon. We had a nice lunch on board and I received orders to relieve my nurses and proceed to Polyclinic Hospital where we were taken in an ambulance by a Red Cross woman driver. Went through a delousing ordeal and I am so tired I can hardly walk. Went to see Eloise and had a letter from Mother.

December 29, 1918: Worked all day and went at 4p.m. to see the fleet with Eloise up the Hudson. Walked from 78th St to 32nd St.

*and Park Avenue to greet Miss Delano at Park Ave. Hotel. Miss
Delano lovely and regal as ever. Eloise thought she was nice. I complete this year back on my home soil, grateful for the experiences
allowed me by the Red Cross. I shall be every so much more grateful
to be back home on the ranch.*

Again Bess was influenced by her friend and mentor, Jane Delano.
When the United States entered the First World War, Miss Delano
created programs of powerful significance to American life. The Red
Cross courses in hygiene and home care were written by Miss Delano
and her associate Isabel McIsaac. The Army Nurse Corps Association's
"Biographies of the Superintendents and Chiefs of the ANC" states
concerning Miss Delano ", *Jane resigned from the Army Corp and devoted her time to expanding post-war domestic Red Cross nursing programs.
She initiated courses to establish and provide skilled nursing care and health
instruction in remote rural regions. Following the Armistice in November
1918 she went to Eu "rope to make inspections and tend an international
nursing conference. Exhausted, she contracted an ear infection and after several mastoid operations her condition worsened. She died April 15, 1919.
Her last words were, 'I must get back to work.'"*

She would have been proud of Bess and the nurses who carried on her
work. These young women and the orderlies who helped them cared for
incredible caseloads of wounded soldiers in their most professional way.

New Year, 1919, began with Bess taking a position as an instructor
for the Army School of Nursing in Fox Hill, Staten Island, New York.
She believed so strongly in the education of professional nurses and
their banding together to fulfill the critical needs of the medical community during this postwar time.

The activities of Bess and her fellow professional nurses truly made
history. The women and men mentioned in the loose papers and the

diaries were referred to often in her notes and in future years as Bess worked with her professional organizations and nursing education.

Trying to solve the nursing shortage, the army, navy, reserves, and Red Cross began to look to other war-torn countries to see how they were meeting the huge demand. England was caring for more wounded in a more efficient method by utilizing the new concept of the nurse's aide. Bess had worked so hard to promote professional nursing education that this new concept was a difficult one to swallow for her.

The army school took a stance that nurses' aides were the necessary link to providing care. From her perspective it solved an immediate crisis but left little in advancement opportunity for the aid herself. Jane Delano had expanded the Red Cross nursing services in communities, creating a rural nursing service that later evolved into the Bureau of Public Health Nursing. At about the same time the army was looking at training nurses' aides, the Red Cross started the Volunteer Nurses' Aide Service. Nurses like Bess trained these volunteers to take over mundane chores to free up the professional nurse for directing medical care. These aides were trained just in time, as the worldwide calamity of Spanish flu hit the nation.

Columbia Teachers College

*B*ack from the war, Bess realized that her nursing diploma just wasn't going to open the doors in the health-care field that interested her. She again registered for classes at Columbia Teachers College in New York City to complete her bachelor of arts degree with emphasis on education.

The bachelor of science in nursing was not available as it is today. The desire to educate the public in preventative health skills and contribute to student nurses' broader education in disease and infection prevention was her obsession and focus. The diary of this year reveals the points of interest that Bess felt were important. Notes from her program are as follows:

B.S. Degree from Teacher's College, Columbia University. (2 yr. course, Major: Sociology) Assignments:

- *American Education by Andrew S. Doper "Mr. Droper is frankly Democratic, makes no apologies for ignorance because it is well to look for knowledge and capacity because they are poor"*
- *History of Nursing: Noting Hebrews & Greeks & Ancient History:*
- *Egypt: Religious interpretation of dreams. Great knowledge of drugs & preservatives. No mention of Nurses*
- *Babylon: Medication guarded by priests*

Education: 174

- *Private Nurses should glorify her own field. Bring back to alumnae reports of groups of cases and this will give ideas to school which is needed. Instead of interest in low society uses, the nurse to be broader, this will bring about consideration of her by the hospital for her private nurses. Vision makes a leader, such as Dentists, have made a profession of a disagreeable work!*
- *A Nurse must not overlook her function as an educator and how to maintain that, in private homes*
- *Private Nurses need to meet together with a vision as to the way they can do better work.*
- *Private Nurses have a far wider experience with disease than administrators. It may be that the wrong material has been placed in the Training Schools—it is a case of a square peg placed in a round hole.*
- *Impatience is a good thing to expect big things, but beware it does not push over into uselessness.*

NURSING EDUCATION NOTES:

- *Is the church indispensible?*
- *Is the State indispensible?*
- *No! Then take it and use it—*
- *Could we get along without the home?*
- *Make each project better by throwing yourself into it. Oliver Wendall Holmes said, "I go to church every Sunday because I have a little plant residing in my heart and I go to water it."*
- *IMPORTANT!! Write to Public Health Nurse Quarterly STAT, for Denver Women's Club to work together with them getting registration of School Nurses.*
- *READ: Women & Economics by Charlotte Perkins Stetson.*

Expense Account for School
<u>*June 23*</u>:

- Breakfast   .25
- Waist   2.50
- Collars   .50
- Tie   .23
- Car Fare   .10
- Ferry   .20
- Candy   .25

<u>*June 24*</u>:

- Breakfast   .25
- Car Fare   .10
- Supper   .50
- Papers   .10

<u>*June 25*</u>:

- Breakfast   .25
- Boric & Camphor   .25
- Pesinol   .25
- Supper   .80
- Shampoo   .10
- Fruit   .10

<u>*June 26*</u>:

- Breakfast   .41
- Cards   .05
- Stamps   .20

- *Car Fare*   *.10*
- *Two Fair Tickets*   *.80*
- *Lunch for Two*   *.45*
- *Cider for 3*   *.30*
- *Supper for 3*   *2.20*
- *Candy*   *.10*
- *Check Barrel*   *.10"*

An Obstetrics note at Harlem Hospital, Columbia University.

- *If necessary to wean baby, put on milk of animal origin—cow's milk—fats—carbs and 3 ½% proteins.*
- *Human milk—1 2/10 % protein. Greatest difference in formula is in protein.*
- *Use milk with high fat content and low protein*
- *Casein in cow's milk is hard to break up in infant's stomach. Average formula has 4 things: milk, lime water, sugar, and water or barley water.*
- *Boil water for first 2 mos.*
- *Formula: milk 20 oz,. malt sugar 2 oz., lime water 2 oz, barley water 16 oz. , that gives 40 oz. of 4% milk formula for feedings of 5 oz. q 3 hrs= 40 oz.*
- *Studied Obstetrics, Pediatrics, Surgery, Administration of Funds, Equipment, and Statistics Keeping*

October 18. 1918: Lecture by Mrs. Chapman at Harlem Council of Women's Meeting

- *Social Hygiene= anything that has to do with health of body*
- *Started with Rescue work*
- *This is only a symptom of disease*
- *Public Bodies not yet ready to take up this work—so carried on by N.Y. Private Society*

- *Knowledge of venereal disease advanced since 1903. Following knowledge of M.D.'s that those were infections as well as transmitted by the sinning one directly to another, and equally in air.*
- *Hippocratic Oath held this truth back as long as now until finally decided to band together and tell the world.*
- *First Steps toward publication 1910. Drs. formed society of Sanitary Prophylaxis under Dr. Morrow. Perceived that physical acts could not be separated from moral. Problem of immorality must first be solved. A good education first necessary.*
- *Still working on enlightening public about these diseases through lectures and pamphlet*

CONCERNS:

- *Experiment last summer: How to get this knowledge to the men on the street who will not read or hear lectures.*
- *Presence of infections is a drawback to work*
- *Several hospitals do not admit such patients because of infectious character and partly because of old idea that it is a punishment that the patient must take it, but the crime is that patients infect others.*
- *Exhibit opening at Coney Island for Nurses—an opportunity to get consultation with photo as to progression of the disease. In two months 1900 men visited this exhibit and over 500 asked to consult. Over 100 found infected with syphilis. It is quite necessary to find out what the picture shows are giving to keep track of them and send complaint to committees.*
- *Education rests more in hands of women to train children right from the first. Children are not understanding the high purpose of these emotions as maturity is reached.*
- *First responsibility is with parents of children for instruction*
- *Teach problems of childhood and adolescence*
- *Courses for young women—girls 12–16 to be "Big Sisters" of younger girls then educate in small groups.*

Bess held many ideals that may well have been the early foundation for groups such as Big Brothers Big Sisters and Boys and Girls Clubs of the twenty-first century. She observed closely the relationships of parents and children in her family and community. These observations led her to work diligently to promote health education and healthy relationships. Benefits of mentoring appeared to Bess to be extremely important to young people. She felt that parents or guardians were the primary caregivers of children, but values, morals, lifelong interests, and passions were better influenced by mentors.

Bess in her 1919 Ford Coupe at the Lower Place
at Rito Alto ranch in Colorado.

More World Travel

ollowing a year of work with student nurses in New York, Bess was called back to Colorado to take the position of director of public health nursing courses at the University of Colorado. Her reputation as a nursing educator preceded her, and she found her particular focus on educating young women in methods of excellence to be in demand. The University of Colorado sent her to oversee the field service (now known as "clinical practice") in Pueblo, Colorado. She spent two years, 1920–21, with this endeavor.

August of 1921 she was again appointed by the American Red Cross (Miss Clara D. Noyes, Washington, D.C.,) to serve as director of public health nursing under the ARC Yugoslavia, Europe, organization for a year, from late 1921 through 1922. She served in Albania and Montenegro until workers overseas were recalled at the end of the year. This area is now southwestern Europe between Bosnia, Herzegovina, Serbia, and Croatia. The diary of that year is on a tiny datebook with miniscule writing in Bess's characteristic script. Excerpts from that time include the following:

November 6, 1921: All day alone going over reports with Mrs. Morrison R.N. Breakfast at Personnel House, Dinner & supper at hotel. Rainy season has begun.

Monday, November 7th: Gave Mrs. Morrison pointers about teaching classes and went with her and interpreter to visit two Maternity cases. Milo the interpreter was from the U.S. and made a fortune and lost it, has been in jail because defending himself from Comitages Gov. plotters.

November 8th: Nikari Montenegro: Warming. After clinic hours and my typewriting, Mr. Morrison & I called on Russion Drs. family of refugees & met nice Engineer who took us home in the rain but we could not talk to him as he did not know French.

November 9th: Podgoritza: After lunch at Nicari Hotel came to Denilograd in car with Serbian Engineer who spoke good French. We remarked about the good and bad conditions of the day and relapsed into silence. 14 people at Personnel House for dinner. Dr. Beadlle came & Miss Regard RN, Social Worker. I slept with Miss M. at the Hospital. Met Miss Wilson at Resniter on the road to Denilograd and asked Miss McLeod to report at Kolasin tomorrow. . Letters came from Russia and Mother."

November 11th: Cetinje:Ambulance and office work. [Ambulance refers to what we now call an *outpatient clinic.*] *Mill. Bossi translated my letter into Serbian for reading to sewing class*

Carbon copies of typed letters that Bess wrote as reports to her supervisors were included in the files of letters she collected. The following tell of the work she was doing for the American Red Cross:

'Soutari, Albania.
Nov. 21, 1921

From: M.E. Shellabarger, Director, Nursing Service, Montenegro and Albania.

To: Miss Helen Scott Hay, Director, A.R.C. Nursing Service in Europe
Subject: General Nursing Activities.

The nurses in Montenegro who have just begun the new teaching work feel a certain timidity as to their ability to organize classes and eagerly study our few Delano text books in order to adapt the lessons to local conditions.

There is one copy of "Public Health Nursing" by Miss Gardner and one copy of "Scheel Nursing" by Mrs. Struthers that are the most useful books, aside from the "Home Nursing" and these books are being circulated as rapidly as possible amongst the nurses.

If stations were not so far apart it would be most advantageous for these nurses who are beginning the new work to visit a station where a systematic routine is established. A demonstration lessen is often as useful to the teacher as to those whom she teaches.

Two nurses are not well established in classes because taking the place of two of the best nurse teachers who were released.

Cetinje:
There was a reduction to the number of patients in the Ambulance during the two weeks of constant rain, but the classes of children attended even though heat has not yet been furnished and the nurse finds the cold almost unindurable.

Great patience seems the one necessity in getting any part of the responsibility taken over by the people. The girls school is an example where fuel and supplies are not yet provided and the opening of the school is postponed.

The girls class is new conducted at Personnel House because of the cold and insufficient clothing of the girls attending. Our Nurse's Aid has begun the work with enthusiasm and makes home visits where she can take girls from the classes to assist in actual bedside nursing.

The volunteer worker feels that she cannot give her services longer without remuneration. Her services as interpreter and secretary at the Ambulance are so valuable recommendation has been made that consideration is given to employing her to continue the work.

Her interest has been very marked and without request she has made translations that are most useful in the class work.

Native physicians have been most prompt in responding when called to diagnose or prescribe, but there is not a physician in constant attendance during clinic hours.

Kolasin:
The work is disorganized because of the Ambulance being closed a few days when the Physician was ill and one nurse had not returned from leave. Schools are now the center interest in order to leave a permanent activity since there are no societies through which to form classes.

Niksic:
Most satisfactory classes are continued. The pre-natal lessens being given to small groups in the Clinic room where a doll is used in giving demonstrations in the care and dressing of infants. Girls classes are conducted in Personnel House where the limited furnishings of the native home are used in demonstrations far as possible. Follow-up visits are made in the homes, where much instruction is given to mid-wives (not trained) found caring for patients.

Denilovgrad Orphanage:
One nurse is more than occupied with administration and the classes in Health are carried on by the nurse who has also the care of supplies and the oversight of the diets. The girls of the school will be placed in homes within two weeks. Home Nursing classes are being reviewed with a view of making lessons in an Institution carry over to application in the native homes. Classes for boys in Hygiene and also Health talks will soon be starting.

Podgeritza:
A translated letter has been sent at the request of the President of the Ladies Sewing Society for her to read at a special meeting to explain more fully the Red Cross classes available for girls and young women. Places have been made for the nurse in charge of the Orphanage Hospital to organize these classes. Classes are help for the elder girls of the Orphanage in Home Nursing and practical work is supervised in the Hospital department where two girls at a time are held responsible for the routine ward work. There are seldom more that two patients in the Hospital at one time.

Scutari, Albania:
There is a very active dispensary (Ambulance) 9–12 and 2–4 every day except two afternoons each week. The nurses make home visits beside their teaching of every case treated in the clinic and also teach girls classes. One nurse visits Catholic Schools on the two free afternoons while the other teaches a post-natal class. Small groups of natal cases are instructed where a demonstration is possible in a warm room with an infant as subject for teaching care and dressing of the new babies.

A tea was given today at Personnel House in order for the nurses to hold a conference with the Franciscan Sisters of the Hospital and the St. Vincent de Paul sisters of the Hospital.

The Sisters seemed most anxious to participate in working out a means of carrying on the care of their children when A.R.C. is withdrawn. The nurses were all invited to a tea at the home of the French Census yesterday where the Albanian Governor (Prefect), the Mayor, Secretary, and chief representative of the Turkish people and the Priest of the Orthodox Church assembled with the Professors and some of the past Prefects. Great courtesy was shown our nurses who were the only women present except the wife of the Canadian Consul.here has been an answer to telegrams sent to the A.R.C. Station at Tirana within the last four days, thought to be caused by the high water in the river after the long rains. The river can be crossed today and the delay is not understood. If it is not possible for me to reach Tirana because of any complication in travel it may be necessary for me to return to Montenegro and go to Durazze by boat.

M. Elizabeth Shallabarger,
Director, A.R.C. Nursing Service for
Montenegro and Albania

The diaries of these months are filled with days of complicated travel for supervision, cold and wet weather that chilled Bess and her coworkers to the bone, difficulties of interpretation due to language barriers, and only small groups of people available for instruction. Regarding one school visit, she states the following: *"Visited School & Clinic with Miss MacLeod. 100 Children in a tiny room with windows closed & hot fire going. The principal had a bath towel around his neck"*. Bess was dealing with Russians, Frenchmen, Turks, Poles, and Romanians as well as Christians, Orthodox, Mohammedans, and an unusual group of volunteers and workers who needed to be trained in health, wellness, and home care. Her diary continued:

<u>*November 24th*</u>: *Arrived in Durazzo 12 midnight after turkey Thanksgiving dinner at Personnel House. 15 at the table. Found*

two American women at the house and in bed who came in on boat & could find no Americans except Red Cross. I had Miss T's bed & she slept in the dining room. The coldest day I've ever known yet, Oranges are on the trees.

November 29th. 35 Lire per day, 12 days 420 Lire paid Mr. Winfield for board and room while in Albania. Miss MacLain is sick in bed with cold. I have chilled ever since coming to Tirana but am determined not to go to bed. Mrs. Ware, the 80 yr. old American and her daughter come to dinner. My report is typed and in.

November 30th. Scutari: The seventy-five mile ride from Tirana was a hard ordeal today. The river bank had grown to two and built into a kind of ferry run by man power. We backed up to a gang plank in water with the Ford but native women with pack horses waded over in the cold. The League of Nations!! Waited to return on our bank to return on the ferry.

December 3rd: Cetinje Montenegro: 7:30 a.m. left Personnel House in Commonwealth. 8 a.m. left wharf in row boat in rain after submitting passport. 9 a.m. hailed steamer which came back for our boat load of 14. Only standing room. Awfully cold. 12 noon walked mile in mud to Plannitaza Customs, did not inspect. 12:30 left in bus on front seat between two Turks & almost froze on 10 mile drive. 4 p.m. left Podgoritza in Commonweath, fog on mountain. 6:30 p.m. Citinje to defend or condemn base of Miss Macleod.

Sunday, Dec.: Most riotous day. Sent letter to Miss Macleod by Michaela. 10 a.m. Service at orthodox girl's School. 12:00 Slava (tea) Women's Society Grand Hotel. P.M. telegraphed Miss Hay, Miss Rossites & Wilson. 8 p.m. went to dance on a Sunday for first time at Grand Hotel. A gorgeous affair but floor not waxed. Some women in native dress, many evening gowns. Officers resplendent.

December 12th: Cetinje: A very full day besides directing clinic all day. Called on School Supt. & on Elementary School where tiny girl had charge of whole room in absence of teacher. Boys & girls separate. Letter tonight from Dollie & postal from mother. Mrs. Lloyd & Michaela here for lunch. Paid 20 dinars.

December 15th: Podgoritza: Class of 14 women organized in Home Nursing. The Major's wife included. Two nurses told of their vacation experiences after shopping in Vienna & Budapest.

The winter continued with cold and an episode of being snowbound while traveling from one town to another to supervise the clinics and school education programs. Bess often had to stay in private homes and sleep in her clothes in spaces where no English was spoken and no comforts were available. She received a few Christmas gifts from home, and the Red Cross group celebrated the holiday with foods like those from home and traditional decorations. January 7 was the Orthodox Christmas that they celebrated with presents and calling on patients. Mail was received by horseback, and roads and transportation were controlled by Serbian Army soldiers. Rain continued through January, and Bess was busy teaching nurse's aide classes and hygiene in the schools. When the aides were instructed, they took over the school classes and home-care instruction. Later that month they began having accounting problems and ended up with lawsuits over incorrect accounting that occurred in some of the clinics. March found Bess ill with temperature and cough. She stayed in bed a couple of days and then was off again in the wet weather, walking or taking public transportation to her rounds of supervision.

March 6th: Finished my Paris report, very tired 7 should have gone to bed but had to go to Twin Valletich Elite of the city's causes met for tea in a French room & had delicious spice chocolate layer cake & little gold teaspoons, not a flavor of Montenegran Style.

Met the Mayor who gave me a rose. Had a REAL conference with Dr. Dobbins & Miss Akeroyd. Letter from mother & Mrs. Sutton. With Miss Akeroyd called on the M.D.'s at Hospital to make her acquainted.

Conferences all day. Dr. Dobbins, Bill, & Mr. Assingrieff took us to hotel to listen to Bohemian Orchestra and drink champaigne. Miss Akeroyd, Irene, and I sat there in solemn dignity until 11 p.m.

Bess was again ill with high temperature and cough toward the end of March. Several nurses and teachers were also ill. Treatment included boiled water, mustard plasters on their chests, and "tonic" prescribed by Dr. Dobbins.

This experience was all before the sulfa drugs and antibiotics we all take so much for granted. One of the schools was held up and robbed and the thief caught. A huge trial caused rifts in the schedules.

<u>March 27th</u>: Podgoritza A long tired day. Dr. Dobbins even came up to see me without being asked and was even pleasant. Said we would all be released in a month. This town is afloat with persistent rains.

<u>March 28th</u>: Still raining. Going to sit up at home today after just two weeks in bed.

Dr. Dobbins returned to Celinje this a.m. and Dr. Bowden came before noon. While I was sitting up Dr. B. came and outlined in a bombastic way how he would turn over the welfare work to Montenegro by May 1st. A proposition that would take a modern U.S. county five years to assimilate. Miss Frazer and I laughed and laughed (afterwards).

<u>March 29th</u>: Miss Gray was wild with pain last night and finally her throat broke(abscess) and she was better instantly. No doctor

was able to locate the lesion with his knife. The last to try was Dr. Bowden & the Serbian Minister of Health.

But Dr. B's good order of hot inside & cold outside did the work. Sat up by the window today but still weak. Rain continues but as soon as it stops I'm going to Cetinje

April saw the American Red Cross group slowly handing over the work of the clinics and instruction to the local people. Bess was finally well and worked hard on reports, instructions, and accounting of supplies and equipment that were to be left at the sites. There were several parties and dances for the doctors and nurses. Bess had made good friends and hoped to see them after this effort. The workers did a survey of the homes in the served areas of births and deaths. Bess wrote the following final report that sums up her work:

Cetinje, Montonegro
April 14, 1922
From: M. Elizabeth Shellabarger, Director, Nursing Service
A.R.C. in Montenegro
To: Miss Helen Scott Hat, Director, Nursing Service,
A.R.C. in Europe

The summary of the activities since I came to Montenegro the first of November 1921 makes me feel that constructive work in carrying out the Child Health program has been done mainly through the class instruction in Hygiene and Home Care of the Sick. There has been the usual delay in getting Ambulances changed from relief centers to Health Educational Clinics that is encountered when cooperating with the Montenegran people who give much time to social observances before the real work can be attacked. The ARC nurses most of whom had not been accustomed to teaching gave much study to the new situation and organized as well as conducted classes that make a most satisfactory contribution for spreading the ideals of trained nurses.

Work has been carried on with Cetinje, the old capitol as headquarters. Podgoritza is the larger town but Cetinje is the geographical as well as the business center, and therefore the logical place from which our efforts should radiate.

At present only three of the six stations which were opened when I came into the field are retained under Red Cross control. The three most important have been selected as host places for our three remaining nurses to demonstrate in a more intensive way the real aims.

One station of course is Cetinje, then Podgoritza with the large mixed population and Niksic which serves a large isolated district.

Vir-Pazer was closed in November, Denilovgrad Trade School given over to the control of the Serbian government in February and Kolasin after being snowed in all winter was closed in March. Vir-Pazar a small town in a malarial district on Lake Scutari had an Ambulance (Clinic) which was an example of efficiency in serving the people. There was also a large group of women who were instructed in Hygiene and Home Care of the sick, while the whole district was better covered by nursing visits in the homes than in any other station, which I consider a splendid piece of work done by Miss Wilson and Miss Rossiter who were stationed in Vir-Pazar during the summer.

Denilovgrad Trade School was a particularly difficult place because administered by the ARC and having the medical and nursing service covered by the ARC, but Miss Akeroyd the ARC nurse who acted professionally in a most difficult situation in a most satisfactory way is to be commended.

Besides the emergency nursing care in a large school the great problem was the administration and the mothering of the large family, and both the boys and girls have learned much to help through life from the women who have represented the Nursing Service.

The girls of the Trade School were give the course in Home Nursing and the boys were instructed in Hygiene and the care of their own rooms in the exact and strict manner that is accepted by trained nurses. Miss Macleod and Miss Wilson at different times assisted Miss Akeroyd and may be credited with this individual work.

Kolasin as a Red Cross station bore every evidence of the conscientous work carried on during the summer by Miss Dalale and Miss Macleod, but just as I arrived, Miss Macleod was away on her leave and Miss Demale was suddenly called away to her home in Italy by the serious illness of her mother.

Work was temporarily at a stand still because Dr. Bergan who was in charge went on leave before Dr. Bowden was assigned to the station. Dr. Bowden was left permanently in charge and I assigned Miss Macleod to carry both the Ambulance duty and the home visiting when Vir-Pazar was closed so that Miss Wilson could report at Denilovgrad.

Nursing activities were soon cut short when in reducing the personnel Miss Macleod was released to Paris and it was deemed best on account of the station being quite cut off from communication by snow in the winter, not to attempt to provide a nurse to assist in work. The good instruction given in the homes by Miss Demale was continued by Miss Macleod during her short service, and the Mother's Club was turned into a Home Nursing class.

Miss Macleod's demonstrations were followed by excellent lectures which Dr. Bowden gave to finish the course. Kolasin seemed less ready for an educational program than our other stations because the whole district has been in such great need of the actual material aid, much attention was necessary during the winter to distribute supplies.

Niksic is the model station as an Ambulance for medical care for mothers and children under the direction of Dr. Beadles who has found the native physicians not at all cooperative about taking over the work through quite willing to have their poor cared for by ARC.

A splendid group of women from the Woman's Club were organized into a Home nursing class by Miss Christie in the summer, and twenty-six of these women attended regularly and finished the course under miss Rossiter and Mrs. Morrison after Miss Chriseie's release. Women of this type could serve as volunteers in Ambulance duty if the native physicians would consider carrying on the Ambulance upon ARC withdrawal.

A class of young girls from the leading families has also been given a thorough course in Hygiene and Home Care of the Sick and I feel that a good foundation has been laid at this station for the establishment of a constructive Child Health program if we could have time to convince the native physicians by demonstration, of the need in their district.

(Bess continued the report of the communities of Cetinje and Podgoritza, which contained much of the same concerns and accomplishments of the ARC nurses and doctors. Her report summary finished with the following:)

SUMMARY: Ambulance: visitors were trained by an intensive course in practical nursing and home visiting. Two detailed as assistants to native physicians in Ambulance. One detailed as interpreter and assistant to ARC nurse during remainder of service. One resigned when native personnel was given control of the Ambulance. Classes: Classes all finished with the fifteen lesson course except the day students in Girls Gymnasium and the Woman's Club class which Miss Aleroyd will carry on in the efficient manner in which she supervised the Ambulance and later acted in a supervisory capacity.

I feel that we have left a group of the most intelligent women and girls in the area well instructed in Home Care of the Sick and I regret that because of reduced personnel and many changes it was impossible to give a longer demonstration of real Child Health work in the Ambulances.

The Medical work was left in the hands of the native physicians, a trained midwife, and the two health visitors who had worked under supervision in the Ambulance. It is a question whether the health work will be carried on more than the provision of free medicines to the poor so long as the ARC supplies last. But a lasting impression has surely been left as to proper home nursing and the high ideals of trained nurses have been demonstrated to the women of the best class.

May of 1922 saw Bess leaving for Paris, France, to report to the Red Cross headquarters. She received a physical exam and debriefing of the work she had accomplished.

She was able to do some shopping and visit chapels as well as spend Decoration Day at the Arc de Triomphe to the Unknown Soldier. She relives some of her war-duty year. For a month she cared for a doctor's children in Paris (not one of her favorite jobs). She visited Cannes, France, and noted that the beaches were not at all like Atlantic City sand, but pebbled. On June 14 she and several nurses bought tickets to Marseille (at RC price).

They went to Marseille, Nice, and were again freezing cold during a cold spell on the steamer in the Pyrenees. They next went to Monte-Carlo on the train and saw the casino, water, mountains, and wonderful fresh water, unlike Paris's. Then they traveled to Naples by boat.

Her trip home aboard the SS *Patrica* was interesting with stowaways, sightings of swordfish, evening dances, and good food. On

June 28 she noted, "I passed Gibralter for the second time in my life. I went ashore during my Round the World trip in 1903 but this time did not even dock." Bess enjoyed learning about the other passengers. On June 3 she notes, *"Have the passengers about card filed now. Mrs. Rogers rules her husband with a rod of iron & does not allow him to be alone one minute; The Sculptor's wife does not allow him to talk to other women: The Italian Count is going to America to marry an heiress; Mrs Crawford says her fortune was not told correctly when she was told she was deceitful."*

Watching and interacting with people was always one of Bess's favorite pastimes. She played cards, read aloud to groups, and visited with groups of passengers. They docked in Brooklyn at seven in the evening on July 7, 1922. True Bess form surfaced when the Red Cross nurses wanted to take a taxi into New York for $6.00. Bess refused and hired a boy to carry her trunks to the subway for $2.00. She arrived at the hotel to get the last room available and went to the Red Cross office to receive the $137.02 for railway fare back to Colorado.

Back at Rito Alto ranch, now as a US veteran, Bess procured her little plot of "home land" and set about proving up on it. The Homestead Act of 1862 allowed adventure seekers the opportunity to found a homeplace in the valleyed mountains of Colorado. A piece of land was chosen, and the "settler" had to improve the tract with a livable home and farm site. When that was accomplished, one returned to the local land office, filed the proof papers, and received a patent. Usually the plot was 162 acres, and established residency had to be proven. A military veteran who had served in actual war had the right to count military service as time served for the residency requirement. This made this time in Bess's life the perfect time to acquire her little piece of her beloved Rito Alto ranch site. The story is that she had help building a small one-room dwelling on the southeast corner of the ranch below Rafe and Blanche's home. This plot gave her a sense of permanency but caused untold problems in the cohesive management of Rito Alto ranch in the future.

Bess never lost her love of the beauty and majesty of her home at the mouth of the Rito Alto Creek. The following poem was found in her files:

WHERE THE RITO ALTO FLOWS

Stand here with me, in cloudland, where the air is pure as gold;
Where ancient peaks, with hoary heads, loom up so white and cold,
Where nature with a lavish hand, how long ago, God knows,
Has formed a scene that is sublime, where the Rito Alto Flows.
The peaks that guard the rugged range, look bleak, and cold, and tall;
But faraway Mount Blanca is monarch of them all,
Here mountain streams start on their way, fed by eternal snows,
But the brightest one of all, is where, the Rito Alto Flows.
Here, the doubting unbeliever, standing in the upper blue,
Wonders if the Bible story of creation is not true.
Back again in fancy to his mother's knee he goes,,
Hears her repeat the story, "Where the Rito Alto Flows,"
To stand beside her cradle, see her waters roll along,
Down to the winding canyon to hear her deathless song
Is worth a day's hard climbing, to the region of the snows,
To gaze on nature's master work, where the Rito Alto Flows.
The prospector has oft been here the mountains to explore
And all day long with pick in hand has sought the precious ore.
But non have touched the locked-up vaults, where treasures now repose
But the golden key will yet be turned, where the Rito Alto flows.
Here, mountain sheep and goat, unvexed graze on the tallest peak,
Here, the red deer loves to wander, and the eagle whets his beak;
Then gracefully, on outstretched wing, up through the blue he goes
To soar aloft above the scene, where the Rito Alto flows.
Now let us leave the snowy heights, on fancy's wing to roam
Down through the rugged canyon, where Bruin makes his home.
There the coyote's howl is heard at night, and the lion comes and goes,
Where the sparkling, dancing water, of the Rito Alto flows.
There it soothes the aching breast to stray, through shaded gorge and glen,
There revel in sweet solitude, far from the haunts of men,
There the pine and aspen mingle, there man forgets his woes,

And the heavy heart grows lighter, where the Rito Alto flows.
(Written by Frank M. Gihford while prospecting in Rito Alto Canyon August 8, 1903)

More Professional Years: 1920s

*F*ollowing the time at home in late 1924, Bess accepted a position as director of public health nursing course under the University of Missouri School of Social Economy, Saint Louis. This was a training school for social workers. The course of study included Principles of Public Health, Methods of Family Treatment, Community Organization, Child Welfare, and Field Work. She belonged to the Urban League, taught classes, worked with a Dr. A. J. Todd at the School of Social Work, and was a member of the Saint Louis Speakers Bureau. On Sundays she would go to recitals, Saint Luke's supper and chapel, attend lectures at the medical school, and holding several committee assignments. Her favorite activities were teaching public-health nursing classes and hygiene class at the School of Social Economics. Bess worked with a community council on organizing summer camps for children. A typical day was recorded as follows: *"8:30 a.m., Dr. Westhoff's Dental Lecture; 9:30, Principles of Public Health; 1 p.m. Hygiene; 2-3p.m. Seniors; 3-5 p.m. St. Lukes, Phoned Mrs. Gree at Blind School; 9 p.m. Social Work dance at Galinworth Hall. Find a number of colored nurses are in the city. 8 a.m. (next day) Horseback riding in the Park; Barnes Hospital Dance in Evening."*

She lectured on combating TB, did Red Cross inventories for the city, spoke at Jewish Hospital graduation, and served at Swanson Psychiatric Clinic. She enjoyed this association until the state appropriation was no longer provided for the School of Social Economy.

Back west she went for 1925–27, to Cheyenne, Wyoming, where she was offered a job as superintendent of hospital and school of nursing at the Cheyenne Memorial Hospital. Again she supervised the education and instruction of young student nurses, instilling in them her disciplines, lofty goals for professional nursing, and practical skills. She led two classes to graduation and then voluntarily resigned because the board of trustees would not give support necessary to raise standards to meet the requirements to become class A under the College of Surgeons guidelines.

There was no compromising her standards, and Bess was constantly working to elevate every organization with whom she associated to the top standards set down by the national organizations to which she belonged. Filling the work void, Bess took a job with Haskell Institute

Indian School. The high-school classes were accredited with the state of Kansas for post-high-school classes. Bess taught prenursing classes at the clinical site in Pueblo, Colorado.

The next position on the career list was inspector of schools of nursing under the State Board of Nursing Examiners in Arkansas.

She had been requested to return to Arkansas to a permanent position since Arkansas law was effectively providing her with a full-time educational secretary.

On March 1, 1928, Bess records that she joined *"the Statistical Division of Arkansas State Public Health under the direction of Dr. Garrison who is very fine. His wife is a nurse who has arrested TB."* She traveled through Arkansas gathering vital statistics and giving out health information.

> *March 20, 1928,* she wrote: *I wrote Dr. Brown of Kansas State Board of Health that I shall send in my paper on 'Tuberculosis' as a needed training for all Student Nurses, before the annual meeting in April. Also will prepare my talk for State Teachers College at Conway, Arkansas and in the meantime try to get my report ready on the Jr. School Survey, as I travel to other towns visiting other hospitals. Met Dr. Wenger, charge of U.S. Public Health, who talked more common sense in regard to Social Hygiene than I have heard in years. He says the women of U.S.A. can clear up our cess pools by giving attention to this canker sore instead of politics and religious controversies.*

> *March 22:* *Finished inspecting Levi Hospital & went to Colored Hospital again.*

> *March 23:* *Left Hot Springs at 2:34 p.m. after seeing Miss Dorothy OConnor RN at Station.*

March 29, 1928: *From the car windows of Cotton Belt Train to Camden, I see red bird, dog wood, apple and peach blooms and palm leaf fans growing. The newsboy selling trashy magazines went back and got a Bible saying he never offers popular magazines to ladies. I told him the men may need the Bible worse than the women as we have own Bibles. The first time in over 20 years of travel over the globe that I've seen a Bible for sale on the train, of course the newsboy didn't catch the point as to the where the Bible is needed. Many Sawmills here.*

March 30: *El Dorado, Ark., an up to date bustling little oil town. The best dressed women I've seen and shops more stylish than Little Rock. At the nice Garrett Hotel the men are allowed to sit around the front stoop and spit everywhere, most disgustingly, so I left my nice room and moved across the street for March 31, to the Randolph Hotel where two drunk men kept me awake who seemed to have rooms on the same corridor. Noisy until after midnight. Three Hospitals where there should be only one, in a Methodist Baptist Community. Catholic sisters are trying to get a school started and a business woman is trying to say another school of course is only exploiting student nurses.*

April 1, 1928: *Palm Sunday. Went to early church 7:30, a beautiful service in a little white church. Water from street cleaning so clear. Called again at the Sisters Hospital in regard to their students wearing white uniforms like graduate nurses.*

The diaries continue with interesting stories of the people Bess met and with whom she worked:

August 9, 1928: *Dr. Irby, Unit Director of Crittendess Co. at Marion Court housevisited when I was in conference with the personnel that* were at an old brick house on a plantation N.E. of Seyppel. The Birge Place (a river steamer is blowing horn loudly tonight) where slaves were chained to the wall in the cellar before the war. Was an isolated place on the Miss. River where slaves could be unloaded and probably kept long after the war. Place owned by three brothers who lived in disharmony for years. Lived in same house and ate at same table, but always each had a revolver beside plate such a jealous fear ruled them.

When Dr. Shelton passed a lovely pre-war house he told of delivering his own wife and saving both mother & daughter 19 yrs. ago with only negro to give anesthetic when his hands shook so after laceration from use of high forceps that he had to have the old negro woman tie the sutures. After going through this and living happily, his wife's people interfered until she left him and turned the daughter against her father, an irratic temper may have added to his troubles.

Other M.D.'s now say this Dr. gets so angry at Ford car that he deliberately runs it into a stump & tears it to pieces. The Dr. himself says he almost lost his mind when his family deserted but the most beautiful memory he has is the lovingly loyalty of his little girl when tiny. Now he has a pet collie dog trained to pick up baby chicks & carry them to safety in his mouth. This Dr. comes from a confederate military family whose brother is now a prominent lawyer.

<u>August 10, 1928</u>: Father & Mother both slaves. Billy Hancock bought her mother to nurse Miss Ann Bowe his oldest daughter. She used to make tea from mud in a swallows nest, steeped the mud.

<u>April 15, 1928:</u> Paid room bill of $5 the week at W. Memphis and sent $6.25 for two weeks in Little Rock. Turrell, Ark. where I am

tonight is such a queer place a nice clean rooming house with a hostess who seems to look past one when she talks & she seems very much disinterested. The lights all went out and at the lunch Counter Cafe, only sandwiches and no milk as usual so I came back & ate some oranges and cookies in my car for supper. Met an interesting ex war M.D. on the worst looking negro street, but he has been schooled in U of Calif and now has charge of Cotton Plantation work. Dr. Thompson also trained a dog like Dr. Shelton for company. But he drinks.

Two beds in my room of course & a lard pail as wash bowl pitcher but no mosquitos or bed bugs, a poor lame man on crutches is sleeping on the porch at the Cafe and I wish I might give him my netting to keep the mosquitos off. The keeper harshly called him 'the fly out there'. We sometimes forget that there will be a time when the "first shall be last & the last shall be first.

August 20: In Hughes Ark. for three or four days in a nice room at house of widow Mr. C.M. Armestreed who allows me to also use her garage. Mrs. L. Freeman, the registrar, accompanied me way down to Burns and to Seyppel near the Mississippi Levee in and out amongst plantations.

Gaunt mules graze on top of the levee in start relief silhouetted against the sky—as if were a symbol of the part of the south where even the people are so undernourished on wrong food that they are weak. It is hard to keep a zest in living in this enervating summer heat even upon well selected balanced diet.

What must it be when the system has no more to draw from than is produced by self-rising bread, pork, and corn syrup. We saw old black midwife, Elsie Williams on Belle Mead Plantation when we wandered onto the house so as to gauge our remained of the trip.

Old Elsie said "I sure dunno what time it is as our clock just up and busted one day and I hain't knowed what time it is since". Just at dusk we finished our conference over registration of births and deaths with Mrs. Lomar Rogers at Registrar, when her husband the most well fed looking man rode up on horseback. I've since learned that the planters themselves do not look at all weak from a poor diet, but what can the poor tenant do who is always kept in debt to the planter and is so illiterate he cannot keep his own accounts. What about the poor family (white) living up in the hills who have nothing to work with and barely enough to live on and with so many unkept children and so fee household necessities that they are ashamed to ask us in to say nothing of sharing a meal with them. The women are barefoot and all chew and spit tobacco like the men.

August 22, 1928: Sketched the old Burgett house which was used as a hospital during the Civil War. A huge high ceilinged place of 10 rooms, three in the attic, where there are some massive pieces of old walnut furniture. The place still belongs to a woman in Memphis and she was a Burgett daughter and it is leased by Lamar Rogers but non one lives in the house except some negros in two rooms.

The rooms which were once probably lavishly furnished in keeping with the old Square piano is now upstairs broken and dusty beside a towering wardrobe which has seen better days along with the largest four poster I've ever seen. The old negro woman doesn't like such a big house as she's afraid. Visited Emma Blocker, another black midwife, out in the field & lost my fountain pen. I saw Mr. Beck himself, the planter, at his Blacksmith's Ship and we discussed everything from pellegra which he thinks due to filth & to the Red Cross workers who helped his tenants during the high water last year.

He said afterwards the Red Cross asked for $100 from each family and they all gave $5 instead and only three refused so he told them to leave his place. Mr. Beck was a travelling man twenty years ago and saw his chance to make money by buying this land cheap. He cleared it and now has hundreds of acres and has saw mills to produce his own lumber for houses and boats and even own farm wagons made on the place. He raises own beef, gardens, poultry, and honey. Houses are poorly screened and I saw few sanitary toilets so no wonder there is sickness.

August 25, 1928: Forest City, Ark. Up at 5 a.m. to see more people in F.City before making my appointments to meet at Shilow Church 25 miles back toward Memphis. A hard trip and delayed by look-ing up such people as Dr. Card at Hetti, who had only praise for Mississippi & her health laws & will not help keep the few laws of Arkansas. Again dark and front tire blew out at Cherry Valley, but just in front of a man and boy on road who were looking for ride into town so they helped me change wheel then I took them the two miles back to town where I bought new casing for $8.50 & came on to Jonesboro where could get good food and a good bed. A glorious moonlight drive and no more car trouble.

EVERY DAY IS A WONDERFUL ADVENTURE. In true southern fashion yesterday I was called "Miss Elizabeth" by a strang-er who saw my whole name on a check. Met a colored undertaker who remarked about Hoover & Curtis as Presidential candidates. "picture looks as he ought to be President but then he is a mixed breed (Indian) and Hoover is straight ango saxon & they always get there.

September 12,13,14, 1928: Health Conference at Capital, Little Rock House of Rep. meeting room. Made the friendship of Miss

Mildred Smith from Minnesota who came to give an address in rep. from Society of Prevention of Blindness. She brought recent news from New York. She lives in Greenwich Village near where Eloise used to live.

October 3, 4, 5, 1928: Entertained at home of Miss Annie Sue Patello who lives with her father in a beautifully furnished 20 room house, worked hard 9–5 for two days weighing and measuring babies at clinic then Sat. scored the cards and spent Sat. night with Mr. and Mrs. James Patello. Started early Sunday morning, went to church and communion after a fifty mile drive to Pine Bluff. Inspected the Jr. School again under Miss Collins, it is so much improved since the spring. Arrived Little Rock tired but ready to pack to go to Mammouth Spring where I went Monday the 8th and stayed with Mr. Stannard to finish up the three counties.

We went to revival in the evening which put me to sleep. A chance for Missionary Board to get back off really trained modern medical young men and send them to the Ozarks to demonstrate use of real surgery and send Home Demonstration Agents to show people how to cook and what to eat and rid this section of pellagra and trachoma where they sell their cows and have no tomatoes or fruit. Just saw a gentle woman lead a blind trichamotous woman to the gate to get into a rattletrap car. Here are honest, kindly Americans in need.

November 9, 1928: 8 a.m. Dr. Hall went with me in my car to see his typhoid pt. and to direct me on the rough mountain road.

A front wheel came off on a good stretch of gravel and driving so slowly it hardly jolted us. Dr. Hall walked to Brewer, a mile farther on, to see the patient while I cleared the road around my car that wagons might pass. He brought back a man who had no spindle bolt to supply them, then they both walked five miles to Edgemont and the car man got the extra part and put the wheel on and I was ready to start. In the mean time walked four miles to see the registrar reported by her neighbors as an "infidel" considered wealthy with 1000 acres, some cattle, goats & 15 fox hounds in the gray timber wolf country. Living in a shell of a north Arkansas house with unsanitary toilet perched on a rock. A girl from P.O. acted as my guide and we ate persimmons as we walked through the gorgeous autumn foliage. Drove back to Edgemont over terrible road after dark but should have remained with the young mother who had a sick baby if I had realized her husband was gone to the Oklahoma oil fields. Finished seeing doctors and registrars in Cleburn County and returned to Bee Branch after dark to get out of the district before a heavy rain which seemed to be coming. At Bee Branch the hotel was most primitive but clean & a little boy had burned ankle which I dressed. Saw contact case where a mother had died from tuberculosis.

Went out to see a registered nurse who lived far up a mountain and acts in capacity of a midwife. Climbed over other rocks & found another midwife not at home. Sunday remained in bed nearly all day, completely exhausted, particularily after being wakened at 3 a.m. by fearful quarrel of people in room beneath me.

<u>November 13, 1928:</u> The old M.D. of the place we stopped next wished me to diagnose his own child's arm paralysis when he found I was from Bellevue. He himself REALLY believed that it was "marked" by the mother's seeing a crippled man. Even in this day and age a M.D. believes this antiquated theory!!! For supper last night the table was laden with hot biscuits, fried pork, boiled cold beef, honey, blackberry jam, huckleberry pie, sweet spuds, gravy, beets, heavy fruit 'pudding' and white bread with syrup.

Mother has written from Canon City where she is with Walter that she is longing to get back to the Valley. She is lonely when Walter is gone on cattle buying excursions. Uncle Ed wishes to make her a visit from Ill. but will not have Pet who must stay with the sick Mother there. Invaluable opportunity in Little Rock for chief to have periodic Conferences with worker and learn from their experiences and suggestions to make service perfect example. Every one to report on hotels & get kitchens or tea kettles substituted for pales of water and common dipper.

December 6, 1928: When driving alone there is such a quick succession of hair breadth escapes in steering between rocks and steep grades when up a higher hill wondering if with all the gas the car will make it. This all makes it impossible to recall the many wonders and thrills of the trip. The first question put to me nearly every town when I seek directions is, "Traveling alone?" "Yes", "Have you ever been married?", "How old are you?" and if I wish to call a certain person, "You a relative of his?" Dr. Watson said I should answer the people who ask how old I am, that I am not yet so old that my eyes have turned grey!

Arrived at the capitol just before the Office closed & told Dr. Garrison I must go to St. Louis to see Dr. D.P. Blair. Dr. G. wants me to remain & will increase my salary but I must give up field work. I am very happy in this work everyone is so nice to me but it is so cold and wet I cannot continue.

Bess went back to Saint Louis and consulted her previous physician, Dr. Blair. He was considered to be the best facial surgeon in the United States. He advised surgery for repair of old x-ray burns on her face and took three pictures by his artist. She consulted the Veterans Bureau Hospital at Jefferson Barracks. They would not be able to have Dr. Blair because he was too expensive. She took on four private-duty cases while she contemplated the surgery. She had just gotten started when Eloise wired that David had the flu and she too was in bed in Salida. They needed the family nurse's help, so she gave us the private cases and started west to care for family. She drove day and night, through Christmas Day, and arrived in Pueblo, Colorado, to find Walter also ill. Bess went out and fed Walter's cattle and then returned to assure Walter's care in Pueblo. Her mother was miserably sick at Canon City. She moved Walter back to care for their mother and then drove on to Salida, where Eloise and David were in Rio Grande Hospital with the flu. She spent the rest of the year driving icy roads back and forth across the mountain to care for one family member or another.

Bess spent the early part of 1929 between Colorado Springs, Pueblo, and Salida assisting Walter, David, her mother, Eloise, and Ruth, who all had one health issue after another. In May, she took her mother and went back to Saint Louis to have the suggested forehead surgery. She decided in favor of Dr. Blair and not the VA hospital. She entered Barnes Hospital on May 10 and had surgery May 11.

May 11, 1929: *Operation on forehead, awfully sick for 24 hours. Nurses gave me no care, and all are graduate nurses.*

May 12, 1929: *Mother's Day in severe pain.*

May 13th: *Raining still & both eyes swollen & black so will not try to leave hospital at least until night. Nurses all gracious except one cheerful little student and some preliminary students. The graduates all seem disgruntled except Miss Phillip, head nurse. This proves it is bad system to have graduates assigned to bed making & baths.*

These nurses seldom think to pull a curtain between beds and one might as well be in an open ward. A friend phoned to learn if she should bring anything to me, I asked for a pencil, but the nurse said they could give me one, and once again she promised it but not *here yet after 24 hours. The attendant does not clear stands & beds thoroughly. Just one row over, the colored ward sweeps fairly well. The doctors & five interns are most intelligent & considerate. Upon admission I paid $31.50, then to 4 bed ward to bed then given 2 white tablets, then intern gave hypo of phenothaline to find output of kidney because I could not produce a full size specimen. Then I drank nearly a whole pitcher of water. The intern took blood from finger for white & red blood count. Then another made chest and heart & slight physical exam. In morning another Intern or Lab Tech, took blood from right arm for Wasserman test. No breakfast, hypo of Morphine & atropine.   One patient did not report so I was rushed to op, room two hours early. Then at last minute Dr. Blair decided to do the radical operation so ordered the Intern to shave half my head then under local anesthesia I underwent the awful ordeal of having skin cut all across my forehead. A huge bandage with blood, hair & hair pins & adhesive made a stiff mass at back of my head, then 24 hrs. of misery coming out from local. Called for the nurse the 2nd night once when I awakened in severe pain & temp 100 degrees. She responded with attitude that I had committed the unpardonable and said I was bleeding behind ear only a little and gave me morphine by mouth & never returned to see if I bled again, telling me to call her if it did start. As if I could after having skin deadened with a sedative. "My Kingdom for some Student Nurses". Last thing before operation Intern had me sign statement to not prosecute 'if operation left me in worse condition than am at present'. After it was all over Sunday about noon another Intern took my complete history & I summarized my several operations, x-ray burn, tonsillectomy, removal of polyp, & others.*

There was so much noise from Drs. & Nurses talking in the corridors until and after 9 p.m. The chief nurse would be dismayed if she knew of this. The head house surgeon took my letters to post them because I feel that the nurses are all to much occupied to be irritated with such trifles. *The pencil which was promised by two different graduate nurses never materialized, but where have I found it? One could never guess, in the spoon holder of this most unattractive room I have engaged.*

I left the hospital Tuesday for a brief lull of three weeks between operations. The bandage on my head is so huge I can hardly put on my dress. It is quite certain I shall need no hat this summer. When bandages changed at Dr.s office he expelled two blood clots. Wore bandages longer than needed because shaved head looked so bad. Had series of wet dressings daily to promote healing. Rafe and Blanche returned from Annapolis having left Martin there for the Academy.

June 25, 1929: *Operated again to complete procedure. Flap grafted from leg. Dr. Blair away so Dr. Brown did surgery. Dressed daily at Barnes Hospital.*

July 6, 1929: *When asked, Dr. Brown said laboratory microscope showed I have cancer. I respect him for honesty. It is removed, but flap and graft needing care.*

July 20, 1929: *Head dressed by Dr. Lewis and more sutures removed. I cannot walk, left leg so sore where skin was removed for graft. Sea sponge and iodoform dressings used. Had Occupational Therapy.*

It took until early October for the forehead to completely heal. During this time Bess went to work as the educational director at the colored hospital of Saint Louis. She found the colored student nurses not as eager to learn as the white or Indian students she had taught. There were some students that were very bright, and Bess devoted extra time with them and encouraged their progress and excellence in care. The final corrective surgery by Dr. Blair (who had recently been declared "top plastic surgeon in America" at a plastic-surgery conference) was done in mid-December. Bess packed her car following final dressing changes and, with her load of Christmas presents for family in Colorado, took off over snow and ice for Christmas at Rito Alto ranch.

The Midlife Years: 1930s and 1940s

*A*ttaining the midcentury mark in her life, Bess found interest in living and working in varied places and positions that utilized her expertise. During these years she appeared to be always looking for the next job to be more satisfying. Arriving at her fifties with the reality that she would not have family of her own, she enjoyed the involvement with her nieces, nephews, and younger family members. She felt her contribution to their lives could be exceptionally meaningful. During these years she also made meaningful contributions to her professional organizations and to carrying out quality assurance and regulatory functions that she felt would make a difference in the way the nursing profession was practiced.

Bess returned to Arkansas for the remainder of 1930 for a second survey of nursing. That finished, she joined the Texas State Board Drought Relief for twelve counties, out of the Brady Texas Center.

Houston, Texas, was home for Bess in 1932 and 1933. Her mother, Abigail, spent New Year's and the winter months of 1932 with her while Bess worked as an office nurse with long days and on-duty time. Abigail had a difficult time realizing it was winter, even with the wet, cold weather, when letters from home in the Colorado Valley told of thirty degrees below zero in January.

The mother and daughter moved twice in January from one cold apartment to another and then to one with a gas stove for heat. They moved by taxi since Bess did not have a car at this time. Abigail even shopped for groceries by taxi. They both enjoyed time at the library and checked out numerous books weekly. Bess continued to attend frequent meetings of nursing organizations, Women's Club, and the Red Cross. Her January 13 diary page states:

"Went to see Miss Mary Kennedy RN at Faith Senior Home then Mother & I went to a picture talkie show to see Gloria Swanson. Her clothes a year ahead in style and it was a good skit on Houston's unmarked streets.

January 15th: Sun trying to peep out but streets sloppy. No steam heat used and very warm. Ruth Tudor graduated from High School today in Arkansas.

Ruth came to live with Bess and Abigail, taking the long bus trip from Arkansas to Houston for fifteen dollars. Starting junior college in Houston was the first focus Ruth had. Bess became her mentor in getting credits transferred and getting a course of study started. Spanish and Shorthand were the first courses for which Ruth registered. The three generations of women moved three times in the next month to find an apartment that had three bedrooms for them and provided comfort in the muggy climate. Professional activities filled the days, and keeping up with historically significant events and family activities was always important.

March 3, 1932: I filled a place on the Red Cross Delano Program at the St. Joseph Hospital Auditorium and told of my personal remembrances of this great lady (Jane Delano) when she accepted me as a probationer at Bellevue.

March 5, 1932: The Lindberg baby has not yet been returned by the kidnappers. Ruth drinks her qt. of milk each day and is gaining her weight.

March 7, 1932: Dollie's Birthday: Letter from her that they too are praying for the kidnappers to return the Lindberg baby. Mother is recovering from her bronchitis after staying several days in the steam heated Sam Houston Hotel.

Just after Easter, Otis Albert, who was attending "agricultural college" in Fort Collins, Colorado, drove a new car from Fort Collins to Houston for Bess. She got busy buying automobile insurance and finding parking space for this new purchase. The women had fun entertaining Otis as they had a car and could visit parks and destinations around Houston that had been out of taxi reach for them previously. On April 8, Otis boarded a bus for Colorado, and Abigail "hopped off in an airplane at 8:10 a.m. for $55 to Pueblo, Colorado." This continues,

Ruth and I were quite disconsolate returning to school and office.

April 11, 1932: Went to the San Antonio Nurses National Convention. I left on 4 p.m. bus for San Antonio arrived at 11 p.m. and found my hotel reservation had been given up at 10. I got the sample room with a little girl on her way to Brownsville.

April 13, 1932: A Bellevue breakfast at the St. Anthony Hotel, read my paper at 11 a.m. and such a large audience we had to change to a larger room.

Ruth and Bess moved again, back to one of the apartments Bess and Abigail had shared early in the year. Rent was less, and they had two nicer beds than they had in the three-room apartment. Bess commented, "Ruth Tudor disappointed me so much by dropping a subject at school." Social life and other activities were Ruth's focus, but she did help a great deal with house maintenance, evening meals, and doing some sewing on a borrowed machine. These things were a help to the busy nurse. Bess noted,

Ruth is making a pink organdy dress that is long and much like my graduation dresses of 30 years ago after the years of knee length dresses.

May 6, 1932: Letter from Martin at U.S. Naval Academy that the cruise will only be to Galveston and Porto Rico this year instead of South American where he expected to see my Ambassador friend at Lima.

Apartment moves were not the only changes Bess experienced. In May the office moved to a new Medical Arts Building. Big plans were in the works for an office opening party in a week. Bess sent out the invitations and orchestrated the reception.

May 16, 1932: Bought 10 cent box of strawberries as good as those at grandpa's at Rito Alto. A lovely letter from Mother with one to Dollie from Eloise in New Mexico before the hail storm ruined their crops.

May 18, 1932: Wire from Eloise telling of David's operation for appendicitis at 10 p.m. yesterday at Masonic Hospital in El Paso. I wired my friend Miss Dietrich at once to call Eloise at once in El Paso.

May 20, 1932: Florence's Graduation Day at Saguache. Letter from Dollie who had not yet heard from Eloise. Wired hospital to inquire about quality of care. Sent $50.00 to Hospital and night letter to Eloise.

May 31, 1932: A terrible shock in letter from Eloise that she has indications of breast cancer. Symptoms for 1 1/2 years and I have not known.

June 4, 1932: Ruth finished her special commercial course at school. Immediately packing to go to her mother.

June 4, 1932: All packed by 9 a.m. and Ruth left on the bus for El Paso.

June 7, 1932: Lonely without Ruth & so tired can hardly pack to move back to the cooler apt. on Clay Ave. Moved in with Miss Willard but there is another apt. if we can't manage together. Ruth must be exhausted as she reached El Paso in a.m.

June 15, 1932: Eloise came from Las Curses, N.M. She looks badly, so thin and weighs only 112 & I weigh 111.

June 17, 1932: Making plans for Eloise to be operated. Dr. Patterson and Dr. Milliken say the right breast must be removed (cancer). Very terrible for us to face.

Eloise refused to go for the scheduled surgery and delayed until she and Bess could go to Galveston to see Martin on the SS *Wyoming*. Finally scheduling surgery at another hospital, Eloise had her right breast "amputated." Martin took leave and came to visit at the hospital to provide support during the ten-day hospital stay. Daily trips to the doctor's office for dressing changes and a slow recovery were experienced by Eloise. She stayed with Bess, having several other health needs addressed, and on July 14, Bess noted, "Eloise made last call to Dr. Peterson's for breast dressing. Incision all healed. Says she will live to 100 years." She left for El Paso two days later, leaving Bess lonely and depressed.

The next family event noted was the death of Uncle Ed Wales at his home in Bloomington, Illinois. These family crises took their toll on Bess, and she spent several weeks recovering from a bad throat infection but continued to work at the office after initial symptoms disappeared. She moved again to the next-door apartment in August and seemed more comfortable. Bess was informed in September that Eloise and Wilbur were unable to sell their farm produce. She noted,

"Our blessed little David said he will get a job." September also brought another move: *"Miss Pridgen had her boyfriend's car and helped me move to this lovely home at 308 Hathaway."* Through the fall Bess kept busy with Spanish Classes, Tuberculosis. Association and working with the Texas Nurses Registry to get new nurses registered and regulated for better benefits.

She weathered flare-ups of arthritis difficulty and severe hay fever, for which she had allergy shots. Weary by holiday time, she bought herself a round-trip train ticket to El Paso to spend the New Year with family and friends.

The year 1933 continued with work in Houston in an office and clinic setting, giving occasional professional lectures to nursing groups on public health, and making regulatory progress in organizing nurses.

On January 12, 1933, she notes, *"I gave lecture before the graduate colored nurses tonight."* The next day she writes, *"Started Public Health Class and went to lecture with the class at Jr. College then to Spanish Class."* In February she notes, *"The Nutrition classes revived and it seems I shall send nurses to assist. Medical Assn. asked me to notify State Legislature to fight Chiropractic and Nursing Bill."* She began working more hours with the state registry and visited multiple clinics by bus to help with health instruction and regulatory work. She attended the Austin State Nurses Convention, visited the Negro hospital, and gave lectures, addressed Red Cross nursing letters and reports on a national level, and continued her hours of office nursing. She was nominated to be president of Texas State Public Health Nurses Association and retained her position with the registry.

December 29, 1933: Letter from El Paso Health Department asking me to take position for $140.00 sent air mail.

January 16, 1934: Sent resignation to Miss Kennedy and acceptance to El Paso.

The next month was filled with packing and completing her obligations in Houston.

Februry1, 1934: Dist #9 gave me a warm reception in a parting tribute and a half month extra salary.

February 2, 1934: Packed all day & another party at Texas State Hotel in evening with a big box of candy. I feel like a bride with so many gifts. Miss Hanna gave another gift.

Bess loved being in El Paso with Eloise there and several friends from previous jobs and career experiences near. Here she worked as El Paso City and County health-department supervisor.

February 6, 1934: Eight hectic hours trying to learn my job as Director of Nursing at the Health Dept.. My reception has been so much more cordial than it was in Houston. I think we westerners are more hospitable than southerners.

By the end of February she was actively traveling throughout the area working for public-health issues.

February 21, 1934: Out in Mexican homes with our Mexican Nurse to vaccinate a whole block.

One of her first crises was a measles epidemic that created havoc in the schools and hospitals and among her nursing staff. She gave lectures on health in the schools and again became focused upon the health and family concerns in the area. She was living at the YWCA, where she was comfortable and made many new connections. Staying close to Eloise and family was important, and she visited whenever she could, always coming home exhausted and often with whatever bug the children had. During this time she was elected president of the State Public Health Nurses. She also contributed to her college-club meetings and the American Red Cross and promoted well-baby clinics within her public-health nursing districts.

June 4, 1934: More prayers answered as things better for Eloise. David returned on 10:30 a.m. bus after a delightful house party. Went to 'A Lady for a Day' talking picture show with Miss Moss. It was very entertaining. My nephew Nicholas graduated from college today.

Her niece, Dorothy Tudor, came by bus from Las Cruces, New Mexico, on her first solo trip at ten years of age. Bess took Dorothy to her office and on clinic visits, plus to church and a play. Mentoring the young women of the family was a favorite activity. The proud aunt stated after Dorothy returned home on the bus, *"I miss her so much, a lovely independent child she is."* It was a terribly hot summer in El Paso, seeming much warmer than the Houston summers. On that hot July 4, Bess writes, *"A hot dry 4th & Miss Douglas and I went to the little park to eat our lunch. We were almost crowded out by drunken men. Consequences of the repeal of prohibition I presume."*

Polio was in epidemic force around the United States. Public-health nurses were besieged with cases, and health professionals succumbed to the disease. Bess worked tirelessly to encourage good hand washing and careful techniques that would decrease the spread of the dreaded paralyzing process.

August 6, 1934: No more Infantile Paralysis cases here but 25 nurses in Los Angeles and 43 M.D.'s ill.

August 10, 1934: Not nearly so exhausted as I was yesterday. Pay Master for F.E.R.A. returned by auto saying there were 139 deaths in one day in Cincinnati.

Bess noted several dates when she participated on the radio in public education programs. One such program was an hour lecture on "Health and Sickness Nursing, by Miss M.E. Shellabarger, under Texas Graduate Nurses Association." She also taught public-health nursing to the Masonic hospital student nurses for several sessions. Another prime project was advocating for better pay for her nurses.

October 17, 1934: Notified by Chief that nurses salaries must be cut again to make up deficit. Why always the nurse and never the M.D.'s? The doctors will not always rule!!

December 8, 1934: Margaret Sanger, Birth Control advocate visited Health Department just after Mrs. Rapp, Miss Morgan & I went to a cemetery with row upon row of infant graves.

From 1934 to 1936, Bess enjoyed this job. Several times a month, she attended professional meetings and conferences, always encouraging other nurses to be involved in their organizations. She would drive her old cars through storms and often at night to arrive at a meeting to hear or present a talk and then drive back home to be back for morning work hours. It appeared to be her practice to drive at night, stop to sleep in the car for an hour or two, and then drive on to meet her obligations.

As noted years later by family members, she always outfitted her automobiles with all sorts of emergency equipment and supplies to be prepared for any difficulty (which she frequently experienced!). Her car trunk held extra water, emergency food supplies (sometimes Eagle Brand condensed milk or powdered milk), several pairs of cotton gloves, bags of rolled bandages, her wartime nursing kit with syringes, medication tablets for pain or water purification, scissors, tweezers, forceps, magnifying glass, suture equipment, extra stockings and shoes, paper bags, soap and washcloths, jumper cables, and other miscellaneous supplies. It appeared she could establish her own Red Cross emergency station out of her car. She would have fit in well with current-day "preppers" who are ready for any emergency.

Holidays at the end of this year were spent with family, as usual, which was a favorite time for Bess.

January of 1937 found her tolerating the cold at the ranch. The diary chronicled her lifestyle:

January 3, 1937: A little snow & very cold. I sorted very old letters all day. Rafe came for supper.

January 6th: Bill stopped with us for dinner. Spilled coal oil from small stove when I moved it. Bill was hurt by cow this a.m. and could hardly eat lunch.

We washed all day & Mother did her own washing (at age 82).

January 13th: Spent the night at Rito Alto then packed my belongings to put into car. Mrs. Roberts went with me to sheep camp to vaccinate Mr. Martinez.

8 degrees below zero and car frightened sheep. Left Alamosa at noon (on the 15th) & over snowy pass reached Colorado Springs in time for conference with Chm. of V.N.A at 4 p.m. Grand View Tourist camp owned by friends in Moffat has gas heat. Half sick with pain in side. Went no place and repacked my cases.

January 18th: Had conference with Director of Official Registry, then interviewed girls at camp. Then on toward Denver & called to see Hugh who is ill at Castle Rock and stayed with him.

January 20th: Had a time starting car after leaving in open all night. Went to Littleton to find Jessie Shellabarger and she went with me in the cold on some errands. Went back to Castle Rock and stayed with Hugh & Lulu after seeing youngsters of the family who were in Denver for Stock Show.

January 30th: Left in the evening for Salida then Mannitou and South Park. Very cold & dark & I removed a tire & tube rather than have it changed. Left car to be greased at Salida & walked to Mrs. Davis' for room. Bought vulcanized spare & tube for $6.50. Arrived in Aspen at 9:30 p.m. after fearful trip over pass and primitive road. Slept part of day at hospital and got uniforms read.

February 1, 1937: New job at Aspen Hospital. Very cold but the hospital almost too warm. Have several cancer patients. One sent to Denver General in Denver. Wet snow all day, gave up plan to see ski course.

February 8th: Still warm and snow plows make road passable. 16 yr. old Emphysema case died, the boy went to school too soon after fly and got pleuresy. Worked on uniforms mother sent from ranch. Wearing uniforms I had at St. Marks' 20 yrs. ago. (just shortened them)

Bess spent the spring in Aspen, trying to cope with the snowy and slushy roads, changes of schedule, and long shifts. She finally chose to take just special duty cases that she could care for one-on-one. This suited her endurance better. She joined a ski club, walked to town to church and civic events, and went to a book club and several book reviews. She seldom drove her car due to difficulty getting it out on the street and navigating the wintry streets. Just about the time a good thaw came along, it was followed by heavy snowfall and messy streets again. She found living in this small town and the hospital situation not to her liking, and on April 1 she again packed her suitcases and left Aspen. Back in the San Luis Valley, she had nice visits with her nieces Jeanette and Julia and sister Dollie. Nephew Alan fixed her car.

She received a wire saying that her Castle Rock friend, Hugh, had died, so she went up to Colorado Springs and Littleton for the funeral and visits there. She spent time with her mother and family in and around Alamosa and enjoyed springtime in the valley. Helping her elderly mother keep up with activities, staying with several neighbors who had health needs, and taking care of longtime friend Mrs. Coleman until she died kept Bess occupied and feeling productive.

June 1937 saw her back on the eastern slope of Colorado, attending a nursing refresher in summer school in Greeley, Colorado, and then accepting a position with the National Methodist Sanatorium for tuberculosis as a supervisor of nursing in Colorado Springs, Colorado.

December 23, 1937: Left Colo Spgs 4:30 p.m. with Miss Marchum. Stayed the night in Salida. Took hot house flowers to Rafe for Saguache. Dinner with Mother, Bill, Otis, Rafe, Will and girls.

December 25th: Will and Janette got Xmas Dinner of turkey for Alberts.

December 26th: Left alone in car at 11:00 for Salt Lake City. Dinner at Blanche and Julia and Bills in Saguache. Arrived Montrose, Colo 8:15 p.m.

December 28th: Left Belvedere Hotel in Montrose at 8 a.m. arrived Salt Lake City 8:15 p.m. over icy Helper road.

December 29th: Went on duty at 8 a.m. and Miss Harden turned over books. Terribly tired. Miss Hardin left for Pueblo and I feel I was given a dirty deal in turn over. Miss Jacobsen went over the hospital work and went on night duty.

December 31st: Had breakfast in room. Emma Selch called up from downtown and I met her at 2 p.m. and out to University in car with her and Miss Wellman RN to make plans for students with Dr. Raines. On duty till 1:15 a.m.

Bess began the New Year back in Salt Lake City, meeting the student nurses and coordinating with the university for classes. She taught, worked full shifts, met many new nurses, and joined the Ogden League of Nurses.

January 14, 1938: Lovely day at St. Marys of Wasatch Academy and took six students to St. Peters Chapel.

January 17th: Preparation for speech tomorrow.

January 18th: Capping exercise. 20 girls at St. Peters Chapel. Pt. fell from a window today. Saw Health movie on pneumonia typing with Miss Wellman.

Jan. 20th: Invited to go out to ski but will go tomorrow. To gym with students then to University Biology lecture in Kinsbury Hall.

Bess followed her group of students to graduation in June and then kept no diary for the rest of the year. From notes and letters, it appears she continued with duty at Saint Mark's Hospital through the summer and fall, noting that she saw Emma and Charlie Selch occasionally until their move from Utah to Steamboat Springs, Colorado.

January 1939 found Bess accepting a job at the Homelake, Colorado, hospital in the San Luis Valley. She was developing diets for nearly two hundred VA old soldiers, sailors, and their wives that came for treatment. She had charge of caring for "cottage patients" and having diet table specials and noted that all were losing weight. She felt she might become popular as a "weight reducer." She made note that Dr. Clark's visiting son looked "like a movie star." She enjoyed playing the piano in the recreation hall.

Bess received several letters of interest from a Hotchkiss, Colorado, job and began considering the change again. Being in the San Luis Valley renewed her spirit, but she became restless. She noted at Homelake,

Dr. Anderson sees 13 patients a day. A heavy load! I moved to a warmer room ($5.00) in the home of Mrs. Hauser. I froze my ankles in the previous apartment. Dealing with Board of Commissioners at the Hospital. Had a long distance phone call from Secretary of the Hospital Board in Hotchkiss, Colorado urging me to accept Superintendency of the Hospital. I want to wait until Civil Service grade comes in here.

Our latest patient is the head painter who is wildly alcoholic and demands his buddy from France to come talk to him. Dr. allowed him out of room and watched by 'another patient' who left him. He ran off to town in dressing gown and slippers. He was caught after walking two miles, and was taken back to the hospital.

More urging from Hotchkiss to come over there. I asked that there must be enough good nurses at all times to run the hospital properly if I am to supervise. I feel I cannot leave here due to severely

ill jaw case (from a tooth extraction) who may not recover and needs my care. Administrator here will not give me time off to visit ill mother, so considering Western Slope job.

After the case under her care recovered, she left that job and went home. While back in the San Luis Valley, her diary had interesting updates on family and her life there.

- *Charlie Bill has another ear infection.*
- *I was working with an interesting, well trained ENT MD with only 12 patients at the office and he is seeing the baby.*
- *Otis & Nell are going with the baby to Ft. Collins for Otis to study for 4 months.*
- *I helped at the hospital with Dr. Clark's surgery, a mastoidectomy on a 21 month old. The father had the same surgery several months ago.*
- *Mother is ill and asked Dolly to have Dr. Shippy see her.*
- *Jeanette serious about going to Japan. Sent her books on diets and customs.*
- *Great News!! Bill is to be married to Marie Hanfeld at St. John's on 2/3/39 & honeymoon in Old Mexico.*
- *Just as I was putting my hat on to go to lunch a man asked if I were 'Bess'—when I answered affirmatively he said he was 'John Lloy'" and that my sister had told him where to find me. We had lunch and he took me to a picture show.*
- *I always need my good strong cup of coffee in the morning or I feel almost ill all day.*
- *I'm taking a Spanish Class.*
- *Alan visited from Western State, to play basketball.*

<u>*March 24, 1939*</u>: *Letter from Mother saying Martin & Betty have a new daughter in Coronado, CA. This was my last day at the Dr.s Office. Dr. gave me a third more than my contract. He's a good man*

though more interested in physics than medicine. I Spent Easter at San Luis Ranch with mother there. Rafe & Bill came in for meals. Blanche is in Saguache. I am cleaning house trying to find my gold baby pin to send to Martin's baby girl who is named Elizabeth.

<u>*March 31st*</u>: *Very lonely out here even with much to do. Planted sweet peas and morning glories. Do go to Eastern Star, Nursing Bureau, and water color Art Classes. Emma and family visited the ranch to pick up Little Ralph who was there a week to help out. Rusty, Bill, & Martin came to work with cattle then left for fishing with camp outfit into the mountains. Just heard Jeanette is going to Japan. Eloise & I had flu!!*

ELIZEBETH SHELLABARGER 1939

<u>*February 23, 1940*</u>: *Wired Hotchkiss Hospital my Acceptance.*

Bess moved to Hotchkiss, Colorado, having a room at the new hospital, and took on supervision of the new general hospital. They must have assured her of adequate staffing for the responsibility she was to undertake.

March 22, 1940: First baby born in the new hospital. Young mother and child had many visitors who thought me exacting because I made them wear masks and not go very near the baby. Spent Easter with family at San Luis Ranch. Mother has sold Rito Alto Ranch to Bill.

April 1, 1940: First baby case went home

April 6, 1940: Called in at midnight when a cosmetologist and her intended were bringing in a weeping infantile paralysis (post) patient who called them to take her to the hospital in a hysterical state. Hernia Patient admitted. Doctors did fairly good "herniotomy" with local anesthetic

June, 1940 It's June and Rafe and Little Ralph are going up to the mountain sheep camp Miserable day alone at the hospital with 2 patients. The insane drug case returned—threatening me. A burn case returned and also a serious heart case was admitted. It really is not safe to have patients in this hospital with no one to help us women when mental cases are loose in town.

Went up to Denver for my annual Physical Examination at the Veterans Administration Hospital.

A diary in the middle of one case was very dusty with just jots of information. Bess found it interesting to discover that was how she lived that year. She apparently did not stay in Hotchkiss long because the diary has her back in the San Luis Valley. Life kept a fair pace, even though she wasn't feeling very "professional" that year. Family needs were so important to her, and she really felt she should be home to help. Nell and Otis had their hands full with baby Charles William, and the winter "bugs" just seemed so hard on that baby. Mother Abigail was ill in Moffat and needed frequent help. This diary helped Bess remember bits of that season:

- *Charlie Bill recovered from Otitis Media (nasty ear infection). I cared for him while Otis & Nell went to the Baptist Church. Dollie & Alan came by. I went to the Methodist Church in the p.m. I am so attached to Charlie Bill.*
- *Jan. 1st: Moved to the place by Otis & Nells 814 Main Street in Moffat, CO.*
- *Working in the Doctor's Office in Alamosa. He is a well trained Ear, Nose & Throat MD—We see 12–15 patients per day. One family in 3 has Otitis.*
- *New Priest at the Episcopal church. His clever wife had made his robes & vestments. He baptized 3 children this week.*
- *Snowed several inches—It is such a cold winter.*
- *Cared for child hit by truck in front of the office. Dr. Anderson was run into by a car near the hospital!!*
- *Pet is getting lonely in Chicago*
- *Staying in "barn like" room Nell and Otis left me in—I really want a better place. Eating out and combinations of starches almost makes me ill.*
- *Treated little boy from Creede with one arm who fell from his "Wheel" and fractured the base of his skull. Also 12 yr. old girl that I sent to the hospital. The boy's mother told me of Mrs Major, who still lives in Creede---she is now lame from a fractured hip. She entertained me with her nieces when I was 17.*
- *Young man came in for a physical for the Air Force.*
- *I was invited to join University Women's Club. "*
- *I am enjoying my Art Class in Moffat and Spanish Class in Alamosa*

- *(March) Moved to another room. $2.50 for the room & they have a piano I can play*
- *Doing some private duty for Mrs. Fennell, a family friend.*
- *Had a severe Cardiac case come in that stretched our knowledge*
- *(May) Julie Alice Graduated from "Aggies" and will teach in Hugo.*
- *"Little Glenn"(Selch) came to the ranch to watch sheep shearing with his Grandpa Rafe*

Not having children of her own, this was the closest she would get to rearing children. Bess truly had little regret that she did not have her own family. Taking care for brief times of these little ones was so tiring and challenging. She could not imagine the energy it would take to spend twenty-four hours a day thinking of someone other than herself. Duty hours always gave her a reprieve when someone else would take over for a while, allowing her rest time to gather her strength. The calling appeared to be favorable for her life and energy levels. Bess did love her family and their children and was grateful they shared their lives with her as they did.

After her time in Colorado, Bess took a job in San Antonio, Texas, working for the Veterans Administration Vocational School. She had three students in her Vocational School Refresher Course. She developed curricula with credentials by the VA and typed out her lecture outlines. These courses included Medical/Surgical Nursing, Psychotherapy, Public Health, Mental Hygiene, and Pediatrics. A Dr. King taught Epidemiology. Bess also taught a ten-hour First Aid Certification course (authorized by the Red Cross). It became increasingly important to Bess to assure that professional and vocational nurses were up to date in their clinical skills and followed all national and Red Cross standards of care for the time. She found so many schools wanting in their approaches to education. Getting able bodies out on the hospital floors working appeared to be the primary focus, but Bess knew the quality of care suffered in the long run if nurses were not prepared for the levels of care that were their responsibility.

The refresher course assisted nurses who had been out of the field for three or more years to become familiar and adept at current levels of nursing competence. She also believed every adult citizen should be certified in Red Cross first aid. That goal still falls short but continues to be a community goal.

Bess taught a history of nursing course at Incarnate Word College during this time. Another belief was that professionals fail to make progress if they are not educated in what went before them. She frequently attended Texas League of Nursing meetings and continuously kept up with the national organizations of nursing and progress of other states. Along with her preparation for her teaching, she was reading to take the US veterans medical exam.

July 14, 1941: Became ill with gall bladder attack. After several days finally got a medical exam and am feeling better.

August 14, 1941: Jeanette writes from aboard another Japanese ship. At Metrozal State Hospital in Texas 19 Student Nurses died of polio.

September 11, 1941: ARMISTICE!!! We continue to celebrate!

September 25, 1941: News from Emma and Charles Selch that their fourth baby was born prematurely on September 12th. Wasn't due until Halloween. Emma doing O.K. and tiny Alice Elizabeth (my name sake) is in a special incubator in the Steamboat Springs Hospital. I probably cannot be of any help.

November 14, 1941: *Went by bus to Austin. Met the bus on 11/19 for Dorothy's visit. Involved in church bazaar, attended Philippino Missionary Meeting and Bible classes. 11/20: Dr. M. Cooper Nix gave Psychiatry Lecture to my Refresher class.*

December 10, 1941: *Black out after Dark. Made students and other nurses very anxious. I am doing occasional Private Duty and St. Marks Hospital and this was one of the nights.*

December 12, 1941: *Did Radio Broadcast for Red Cross and had a card from Herbert Hazard that they heard my radio broadcasts in Saguache.*

December 24, 1941: *Went home for Christmas, arriving in Moffat before midnight. Rusty & Florence Britton were there. I gave the family a movie that we watched at Dolly's. Sunday dinner at Rito Alto with Bill, Marie, and little Gretchen.*

December 30, 1941: *To Blanche and Rafes, Rusty and Florence stayed all night there. VERY COLD. Rafe & Rusty took me to San Luis Ranch where Otis had the house warm for me and cow gave fresh warm milk. (lasted 2 days).*

January 1, 1942: *Moffat, Colorado, 20 degrees below zero. Dinner with Otis and Nell in their sunny house at Moffat where the front door has 'Waiting Room' insignia. Inside we found Charley Bill running his new track train. Mother and Dollie, Will, Alan and Jeannette (in her pretty red cotton knee length dress, joined us. Nell had a perfect dinner and served buffet—which was most pleasing to everyone. We all love Nell and continue to thank Otis for bringing her into our family.*

My old malady seems to have returned as usual in the high altitude and my head sinuses are so filled and irritated I'm not half par. Went back to San Luis ranch alone for the night since it is too cold for mother yet she would be very happy to go with me and I too because we could read together.

January 3, 1942: Took Civil Service Exam in Alamosa then bus back to San Antonio.

She was required to take the civil-service exam to continue working due to being over forty. She sat the six hours at the exam in a cold room and then on an overheated bus and arrived back in San Antonio with a bad cold. She stated she hadn't had a viral cold since 1922 in the Balkans. This bug seemed to hold on as she went back to teaching classes in history of nursing, home nursing, Red Cross first aid, and public-health nursing at Incarnate Word College. She was teaching graduate RNs how to teach history-of-nursing and public-health courses.

The 1942 diaries hold much history of the war and worry for the family as Alan Albert reported to San Diego and later was assigned to the Marine Band and spent time "shipped out."

David Tudor was at Richardson Air Force Base in Anchorage, Alaska, and spent time in the Aleutian Islands off that coast, and Lieutenant Martin Shellabarger was finishing in Annapolis, on the other coast. G. W. Hicks, Julia's husband, reported for the draft. Everywhere were signs of the war effort. Machinists were being begged to go to Pearl Harbor, federal monies were available for women to attend training programs literally for free, rubber for tires was scarce, and food rations were in place, with collections and donations from every church and organization going to war needs. On January 23, 1942, Bess states,

$25,000 in a check was given by a member of our St. Mark's Church for the Chaplains' Army Fund, this is wonderful, but maybe if a few checks of this order had been forth coming and real enthusiasm

during last 20 years for reaching the under privileged and teaching hygiene and health to the over privileged and the Golden Rule taught between Nations, "Free Trade" for instance, we might have no wars.

March 28, 1942: Another card from David in Alaska the dear boy—still in the Signal Corps & likes the switch board at Ft. Richardson. This information was allowed through even censorship. Little mail gets through from Alan which is such a worry for Dollie.

May saw Bess finishing up her classes and being concerned with news from the ranch that her mother was ill with fever. The needed steps were taken to finish up the San Antonio volunteer work she did for Women's Club, AAUW, Nursing League, and Red Cross home nurses. As always, she was actively following the war news and admonished others around her for taking an unconcerned outlook on understanding what was going on in the world.

Bess wrote volumes of letters to friends and colleagues from years gone by to alert them to the need to keep health care and nursing education abreast of current wartime needs. She feared so much effort was going into the war and local and national concerns were being neglected by those left at home. June of that year brought a message from the Veterans Bureau that she had ten days to arrive in Dallas for her periodic full physical exam.

She had complained of the viral symptoms and severe fatigue most of the spring and knew this exam was necessary. Packing her belongings and shipping some to Colorado, she boarded the bus for Dallas on June 5.

Admitted to the veterans hospital in Dallas in July of 1942, she spent the next three weeks as an inpatient, undergoing every test available. Multiple lab tests, upper and lower GI procedures, multiple x-rays, gallbladder exams with dye, eye exams, dental exams, and many days waiting for results to appear filled the month. No mention is made of why she was undergoing all of these tests other than that it was a required update for veterans administration. During this time Bess read volumes, walked the halls, and "interviewed" nurses and technicians about procedures, visited servicemen and women, and certainly made herself known as a "forward" person. Mail finally reached her with news of family health, and she listened to the radio earphones daily for war news.

June 21, 1942: My regular weighing revealed I've gained 1/4 lb. in spite of missing four or five meals this week before tests. Surprise letter from Eloise on Sunday when I was told no mail comes.

David was moved somewhere in the war area and Eloise presumes to those awful Aleutian Islands that are now under Japanese fire. It is so awful to think of these fine youngsters having to meet the worst enemy that America has ever faced. I WILL have faith that their firearms will prevent them being taken prisoners and I shall always remember the way David's lovely smile tamed the 'wild woman of the desert'. David has probably aged 20 years in experience in these two years since.

July 3, 1942: Chief Nurse called in a.m. with Dr. Roe for inspection rounds when my packed luggage was all on the bed. Miss Ross asked the floor head nurse to sign my release and I was told transportation would be furnished in a few minutes. I asked for pickup truck to take me and trunk with other baggage, they wished to send me in big car but I preferred the easy way to get luggage all at the station simultaneously. The big Guard who drove the car seemed in a rush so I barely had time to say goodbye to the other Vet. patients. Such a crowd at bus station. I could not allow the Guard to wait until trunk could be placed in parcel room. Lunched at Cafeteria and decided to get shopping finished because the entire city of Dallas seemed going out for the 4th. I wish I had remained at Hosp until Monday to avoid this rush. I overlooked the holiday! Spent the night at the Y.W.C.A., was most pleasant

Bess in 1943.

Early in 1943 Bess was doing private-duty nursing at a hospital in Salida, Colorado, while caring for her mother near the hospital. Being close to the San Luis Valley, she was involved in family communications about the war. Concern over the young men who were serving and the many activities that were affected by the war effort filled her diaries. In January the family sold the hotel in Denver that they had owned for years for $10,000. Her mother was able to sign her name to the papers, and it was noted that some days she was stronger than others.

Bess noted, *"N.Y. Soldiers are in town. They break the army mules and many never saw a mule before."*

Another note states,

Picked and sent pints of pinon nuts to David and Alan. January 23, 1943: Patient wants me for private duty again tonight. Mother is better and asleep early. The patient died at 1:00 p.m., so I can sleep tonight. Our Dorothy Tudor pinned the gold shoulder bars of 2nd. Lt. on her Larry at graduation from air school then she met his mother at Lubbock where he won his wings.

January 30, 1943: Planning to go home tomorrow but Mother fell and probably cracked her hip.

X-rays confirmed Abigail's hip was fractured and she was moved to the Salida hospital for care. Bess assured that a radio and Alamosa newspaper were there for her mother's comfort during the long weeks of healing. It was a terribly cold winter, which made travel and ranch duties in the valley more difficult. Dolly received letters from Alan Albert, then stationed in Australia, and David Tudor, who remained on duty in Alaska.

Rafe was not at all well all winter with bronchial difficulties. He was cautioned to not stay in the high altitude and cold, but to Bess's chagrin he ignored the suggestions and just kept working.

February 14, 1943: Opened Mother's half dozen D.A.R., Valley, and birthday cards from Saguache. Quiet sunny day and Mother more comfortable but has fever. Mother 89 years old. I was so dazed from lack of sleep I went to bed when the lady came for two hours.

Rafe & Blanche came from the Valley and woke me up. More cards came for Mother but she was too sick to care.

Letter from Alan in Australia censored out any information on his where abouts. Mother restless with fever and irritation under her leg cast. Will employ 17 yr. old Alma Heckel for 2 hrs. tomorrow to assist with Mother while I sleep.

March continued with Abigail running fevers, delirious at times and not doing well. Bess was wise enough to employ assistants to give her respite with the care. Eloise and Dolly came to help periodically, and Bess noted that Marie was on her way to Iowa to care for her ill mother who had cancer. Eloise stayed from New Mexico and alternated twelve-hour shifts of mother care with Bess. Rafe came in from the valley occasionally and ran errands for Bess and then stayed with his mother while Bess slept a few hours. Abigail was being given sulfa drugs that were some help in controlling ongoing infection and fevers.

Blanche and Florence and baby Nancy stopped by on the way to Saguache from Denver. Rafe had been at the ranch cooking and tending the little calves while Blanche was gone.

Marie came home, and she and Bill brought their two little girls (Gretchen and Katherine) for a call. They had a new housework assistant at the ranch for a time to help Marie. Otis also came up to Salida to help with Abigail's care, and Bess noted he was "good at turning her with the heavy cast." It was noted that Marie's mother died in Iowa on April 7, 1943, at the age of seventy-eight.

April 18, 1943: Terribly tired and Marie was here with infant Katherine so I went to bed upstairs. Dolly came to prepare Mother's dinner. Otis and Nell stopped at night. Five weeks ago we brought Mother from the hospital to the ranch and she now has a normal temperature. Gretchen and Bill came to visit. Julia and G.W. Hicks due at Saguache before he goes into Army Service next week. 1st rhubarb and asparagus from our garden, also dandelion greens. Rafe, Wm., C.W. helped George White dehorn and Blanche, Florence, Nancy, G.W. & Julia called before G.W. reports for Artillery on Wednesday.

Bill Hicks went to Fort Sill, Oklahoma, for duty, and Julia came back to Rito Alto. Letters were received from Alan in Australia. He had entertained the engineers and also had some USO entertainment that came to them. Martin wrote he wanted to *"get into the fun"* before the war was over and expected active duty soon. Eloise had letters from David sending home all but his fighting uniforms and saying he was going far away from Alaska. The uncertainty of war was very difficult for the family waiting at home. Bess planted a large garden and tended it, cared for her mother, and tried to get enough sleep, thus filling her summer.

She was grateful for the daily visits by family members who assisted in cleaning, care, errands, and gardening. Abigail was helped into her rocking chair most days and read current events from news articles. She remained interested in what was going on around her until early autumn.

Again running temperatures, Abigail was bedfast. Bess noted the anxiety and helplessness family members felt when they could do so little to stem the failure of the matriarch's health.

September 12, 1943: Dear Mother's death 9:10 p.m. on a beautiful sunset evening with one evening star and a clear call for me. Abigail Shellabarger's death was from liver complications, pancreatitis with blindness and acute glaucoma. Everyone left at midnight

Rafe, Blanche and I went to Saguache to select casket and remained the night.

A funeral was held on the lawn at Rito Alto, and then cremation was done at Fairmont in Denver. Bess did a few private-duty cases in Alamosa. She stayed at San Luis ranch with her mother's ashes until interment at Rito Alto Cemetery between Abigail's beloved Adam and daughter Emma.

September 29, 1943: *Little Katherine strangled in crib during nap in a new sleeper garment today. To emergency in Monte Vista with artificial respiration all the way but no use.*

October 2, 1943: *Burial of little Katherine dressed in red coat and hood in gray casket like Mother's. Marie looked like Modern Madonna giving up her best as she and Wm, Blanche, & Rafe came by car to the grave. Grave just west of huge Shellabarger granite stone.*

Bess remained at the ranch sorting her mother's belongings and settling the estate.

October 16, 1943: *Jeannette Abigail Albert married at St. John's Cathedral Chapel, Denver, Oct. 16, 1:30 p.m. Fred baptized by Bishop while awaiting Dolly & Will. Her picture as Mrs. Frederick C. Paine was in the Alamosa paper.*

Another tragedy hit the family in mid-October when Ruth Tudor's husband and his father were killed in an auto accident. Ruth had gone right back to work after this loss. Bess was asked to go to Trinidad, Colorado, to take on a private-duty polio case in an iron lung. There was a big infantile paralysis (polio) scare with several deaths. When the private case was ended because the family did not have funds to pay her, Bess moved over to Monte Vista and worked at the hospital there for the rest of the year.

Completing the settlement of her mother's estate and regaining her own health after a difficult year of stress were her main focus.

Bess did some private duty around the San Luis Valley and then moved to Phoenix, Arizona, after a call from a physician she had previously worked for who needed a private-duty nurse. The warm climate appealed to her for the winter. There she stayed until returning to Rito Alto in 1946 to keep house for Otis while Nell and Charles visited Nell's family in Tennessee. Establishing her "home" in her estate-received home on the lower ranch at Rito Alto, Bess contemplated retirement. She decided to spend part of each summer near family in Colorado and establish her retirement home in Tempe, Arizona, where she could be warm and keep her mind strong taking college classes in sciences, politics, or art.

Gary and Dale Tudor, Chris and
Grant Olson, and Bess

Bess original that hangs in home of "Betsy"
Shellabarger Bayne in Albuquerque, New Mexico

IV

Imperfections in a Beautiful Fabric Are Often What Make It a Masterpiece

1950s

The 1950s were a time when Bess enjoyed her "retirement" and the temperate weather of the Phoenix and Tempe, Arizona, area. She continued to move frequently and kept close tabs with neighbors and family members. She complained of the cold in the winter and felt the summer heat keenly. If she found an apartment "down the block" or near the university that had less expensive heat or cooling and easier access or more light in the rooms, she collected a group of friends or students and moved all of her possessions to the new address. Each new address brought her new acquaintances with whom she developed interdependence. If a neighbor lady needed transportation for groceries or errands, Bess developed a bond, and they would shop together. If a student nearby befriended her, she would pay him or her a small amount to help with household chores, in return for tutoring or typing. Bess continued her passion for education, taking one or more classes at the university or community colleges either in the arts or in new public health issues. At least one or two days a week she would attend church and church meetings, Women's Club meetings, or nursing-organization events. Family members from all parts of the family tree appeared in the diary pages as they visited Bess, wrote newsy letters, or reported illnesses for which they asked "Aunt Bess" advice.

Ruth and Eloise Tudor, Emma and Charlie Selch, Alan and Mary Lou Albert, and Nell, Otis, and Charles Albert were in frequent contact with Bess. She kept in touch with brother "Rafe" and Blanche

Shellabarger's travels to and from their five children's homes and seemed to always know the location of most of the extended family and what their current activities were.

Springtime was usually the time Bess would load up her car and head for California for a few weeks to visit the Tudor and Paine families. These coastal destinations were interesting because she frequently noted complaints of the cold, wet climate that made her joints or allergies miserable. Sometimes she would live with family members, but often she found a motel room or boarding house nearby so she could maintain her independence. Being involved with the growing family members appeared to be her emotional replacement for being involved with children of her own. She took a vital interest in the education of each youngster and the choice of college he or she was making. Her support and the encouragement of extended family must have been effective, as second and third generations behind her received their college degrees and went on to successful career paths. Each grandniece or grandnephew received at least an annual letter from Aunt Bess with encouragement and praise for the educational endeavors.

Bess returned to the Phoenix and Tempe area for a few months, and then when the weather became uncomfortably hot, she packed up her car and headed for the San Luis Valley for a time of respite.

She maintained her "cabin" home on the Otis Albert ranch, where she would "nest" for a while. Her many boxes of history, nursing materials, and records gave her the daily activity of sorting and disposing. She found from the many files of records found with her daily diaries, that sorting never really was finished. As she sorted, she would often note that one family member or another would take a box of pictures or folder of documents to Saguache or Alamosa to mail to her sister or some distant relative with a similar interest. Her interest in preserving family history and maintaining knowledge in the next generations was a passion of hers. Bess wanted those who followed her to know from whence they had come and the interests and health histories of their elders.

Bess went from Phoenix to Glenwood Springs, Colorado, in January 1953 to help Mary Lou Albert, who was in the hospital for some time. The family nurse then went on to Moffat because Otis had "flu" and she was fearful that other family members would contract it and need help. She suffered a brief round of flu-like symptoms, but her self-diagnosis was "fatigue and similar symptoms" that put her out of commission for a few days.

She was concerned that Otis had "lumbago" following his flu illness as he was unable to work for a few weeks. While Bess was in Moffat, Mary Lou landed back in the hospital with a "staph abscess" that required RN treatment. Back to Glenwood Springs Bess went. She took notes of the illness progress of each family member in her care and often spoke with the doctors treating them, also consulting RN friends about their care.

Once back in Moffat, she did health examinations at the school. Her connections and experience seemed to make her services appreciated. Throughout the time she spent in the San Luis Valley, she often drove to District Nursing Association meetings and kept up with many visitors and friends with whom she had either worked or served in organizations over her career years.

May of that year had Bess still caring for ill family members at or near the ranch. Jeanette, Janet, and George had come to visit before Memorial Day and came down with measles. For over a week, Bess was up day and night relieving symptoms for one or another patient and trying to avoid the spread of the disease to others. Her diary recorded the following:

June 6, 1953: Will Albert took George and me to see Dr. Hurley in Alamosa, he was gone for son's graduation in Boulder, but Dr. Bradshaw said George O.K.

June 7, 1953: Took George early out to sheep camp shearing and to see Memorial Day Cemetery Decorations we had missed. Hoped to keep him away from Sunday School communicable contacts and Marty.

June 10, 1953: Jeanette had hard chill at noon—Reaction from Penicillin Med. I worked to finish neglected health records at school.

June 11, 1953: Barely made appointment with Miss Pfrummer R.N. State Health Department Rep. at Cripple Children's Clinic in basement of Catholic Church, while Dr. Bradshaw made physical check for Jeanette and Janet. Jeanette ordered 4 days to bed.

Bess began suffering from severe hay fever in late June and decided to return to Phoenix. She took her usual several days with multiple car problems to make the trip back to Arizona. She stated she hated leaving Jeanette still feeling unwell but just could not survive the allergy problems. She spent a long, hot summer in Phoenix (Tempe) but continued taking some classes and attending the regular meetings of her organizations.

September 4, 1953: Fell, fracturing my hip and taken to Veteran's Hospital by ambulance.

September 5, 1953: Long Miserable day after x-ray last night. Dr. Milton put on a Buck's extension on rt. leg which was reinforced by another M.D. about 3:30 a.m.

Bess had surgery on her right hip with an extended hospital stay followed by PT and OT. At one point she stated, "Prayer is making me less impatient." Many friends and family visited and sent flowers and cards, which all had a positive effect on her healing. She finally went home from the VA hospital on November 13.

Several neighbors assisted her with grocery shopping and her process of looking for yet another apartment that would be more suitable, since her current one had a step down in the kitchen that caused her unnecessary pain. Emma Selch came for a week to help her, and they enjoyed drawing and writing Christmas notes together.

The little red diary containing the years' activities of 1952, 1953, 1954, and 1955 had several pages that she stated were "ruined from [her] writing while under narcotic influence."

During three days she wrote about her wishes upon her death, including the wish to be cremated with no embalming, have no age printed in any obituary that might be written, and have her favorite possessions, which were placed in a long list, bequeathed to family members and friends. A later entry informed, *"I cannot collect my senses since the second yellow capsule."* Numerous times over the years, she noted that medications affected her much differently from the norm and she was very sensitive to any medicating.

In April 1954 Bess finally became weary of the chronic pain in her hip and entered the Phoenix VA hospital for a total hip replacement. Daily diary entries recorded this lengthy and difficult surgery and recovery. At that time the replacement was a "Stainless Steel Toadstool," by her description. Following the surgery she was placed in a nearly full body cast from her waist to toes. A window was cut to create an opening for wound care of the incision on her hip.

She reported daily the care, treatments, by whom the care was given, when the doctors made visits, condition of her skin, and activities on the multiperson female ward on which she spent the next five months. For three months she was turned frequently, had her bed moved to create changes of view, and received total bed care. She suffered from some skin breakdown on her foot and spots on her back that took increased care to heal. She did much dictating to the nurses and caregivers concerning care techniques and quality of care. "Once a nurse, always a nurse" was so true in caring for this hospitalized RN.

It was a challenge for the caregivers to meet the criteria Bess set for herself. After three months she was allowed to begin sitting up, the cast was decreased in size, and she began an additional five months of physical therapy, occupational therapy, increased skin care, and emotional support by hospital staff and family. It was a long and difficult rehabilitation period through which Bess suffered great pain and impatience as well as experienced insights. She would later write that the experience opened her eyes to much that a patient must endure. This gave her greater empathy and information that she hoped to share with other professionals and care receivers. During this hospital stay, she lost her rented apartment and by November had to have family assist in finding another bottom-floor apartment in Tempe that would work for her continued recovery and rehabilitation. On New Year's of her seventy-fifth year, she was again "home" in a comfortable setting surrounded by her books, files for sorting, and connections with friends, old and new. The new hip did help her mobility considerably, but she was ever after bothered with severe arthritis and effects of temperature changes of heat and cold. She walked with a limp thereafter and used a cane when out of her home.

The years of 1955 and 1956 were better for her after she finally felt more "whole" and healed. Most of these years in the late fifties were spent in Tempe, Arizona, with short visits to the San Luis Valley for family visits. One diary note, highlighted by an asterick was *"Passed Drivers Test Today."*

Bess started the year 1959 with her escape from Arizona to visit family in California. Having no children of her own, she enjoyed connections with her niece's and nephew's children. It was interesting that she would choose to visit California, on the cooler, damper coast, midwinter, when most Arizonans do the opposite: stay in temperate Arizona in the winter and visit California when the heat gets unbearable. Having made a move to her new apartment, she really didn't settle in before venturing off to visit. Her trips were always interesting, in the planning, directions, and timing of her travel days:

Monday, Jan 8, 1959:"Finally finished last touches in sub. left apt. 10 and car filled to brim & kept promise to stay night at Ruths so as to talk a bit before she would leave at 7 a.m. for office when she would drop Mark on way at his school.

Jan. 9th: Enroute to California. Left Ruth's house 11:45 a.m. after sufficient rest for the road. From Valley Natl. Bank, closed acct. of over $700 in savings to place at higher rate in Western Savings in Mesa, Arizona. $200 in cashier's check for deposit in Jeanette's bank in checking account during Calif. sojourn. Left Phx. 3:15 p.m. & stopped for night at Wickenburg Motel, back of drug store ($3.00).

Jan 10th: On from Wickenburg to Gormain's on edge of Bakersfield, Calif. ($5.00) at good warm Motel and Cafe.

Sunday, Jan. 11th: Rested most of the day in Bakersfield while trying to locate Mr. Timberlake then went to Mc Farlain Motel 2 miles north for night. ($4.00) A nice woman was mgr. & owner. $15.00 in gasoline from Phoenix: Speedometer reading 33,450 miles on the car.

Jan. 13th Arrived in Mantica, Calif. at 7 p.m. & phoned to Jeannette who directed me how to find her on Michigan Ave. Warm greeting from Janet & George.

Jan. 14th: Congested with the cold as fog rolled in and Jeanette drove out in the dark for her position at San Juaquin General Hospital for a big dinner for staff members.

Jan. 15th: I had stayed with the children until midnight while Jeanette went with other staff members to attend Regional Dietition on Public Health Nutrition dinner meeting in Sacramento. Today we all went for the regular Thursday eve. library visit 7–9 p.m.

Jan. 16th: The regular visit to Bank of Amer. in Mantica as soon as Jeanette returned, where I deposited $200 cashiers check then we shopped for weeks groceries which are higher even than in Arizona.

Jan, 17th: George went after dark for Scout trek and I with Jeanette went to Stockton A.A.U.W. 1 p.m. luncheon, then a little shopping & on to see David, Marge, & the boys.

Sunday: I was too too stiff from cold, damp fog to go to church with Jeanette & Janet. George returned before dark, very triumphant with Scouts.

During the Mantica stay, Bess attended concerts, church, and meetings with Jeanette and took care of Janet while she was ill and out of school. Following her usual pattern of frequent moves, she went from the family home to a nearby motel much like the apartment in Tempe and paid twelve dollars per week for rent.

Her independence was worth the cost to her. Bess visited the chamber of commerce for information about local points of interest and activities. As was her practice, she procured a local library card and continued her active reading habits and wrote daily letters to family in Colorado and friends around the country.

January diary notes continue:

Went over to get supper for children while Jeanette remained at Hosp. for entertainment & party by Student Nurses, but Janet & George had all under control and served me with dinner. Letter from my Attny Ellsworth which crossed my letters. Mailed letters— first at the window—then shopped for more apt. equipment. My Rx from Tempe came so quickly. Jeanette & Janet stopped at dark to tell me Dorothy is going down to see Eloise & David & Marge. They expect their new car then go on business trip to Santa Barbara & hope to bring Eloise for visit with them in Stockton. Janet was not well & home all day & none of us knew this.

A day later, she wrote, " Sunshine blessed weather after the fog that congeals everything, me particularily. Mailed 8 letters including to Rafe, also $29 check to Attny. R.F. Ellsworth in Phoenix. Letter came letting me know my license plates in Phoenix will be mailed to Mantica for only $4.00." Bess spent the months of February and March in Mantica, where she integrated herself into the activities of the busy family there. She always enjoyed the civic and professional meetings she could attend in California and being involved with the growing children. The California climate was very difficult for her as her arthritis and breathing difficulties responded poorly to the wet and foggy cool weather.

It was interesting that she did not spend her winter in sunny Arizona and enjoy warmer weather in California when it was so hot in Arizona. But that was Bess, never doing things as others would.

Feb.1, 1959: Out before 9:00 to phone Marge and David at Stockton before they left for work & just after boys had gone to school. Sketched a new blooming Gardenia for a letter to Eloise, then went late so as to see Jeanette as she returned from duty. Example of

₁ᵥₒdern Children: Even my beloved George & Janet said they did not introduce a teacher they knew to me because they feared I would embarrass them. I asked how I'd ever do that. They said I drove too slowly and their friends didn't like that.

Her notes in 1959, while visiting in California, continued:

The U.S. Sputnick is still in orbit and there have been slight earth quake shocks in Santa Cruz. I am glad my dishes are secure in my cupboard. Three weeks of medication and Janet is still on throat isolation & cannot go to school. Jeanette is no happier than I am with the School referred Doctor's negative treatment for Janet. I check on her often and one day we had a wonderful visit in the early a.m. when she asked if I had breakfast? Then she had a bad time because I have only canned milk & she isn't used to that. We danced by radio waltzes then she went to the office and phoned her mother and was again her lovely nine year old self.

March 23, 1959: Getting ready to move back to Jeanette's home so as to look after children this Easter vacation. David came from Stockton with the boys and left Gary to help me pack the car. We all enjoyed lunch at Jeanette's house.

Janet is happy with many bouffant skirts to hold out her dresses—the violent style at the moment. She will not allow other children at school to see anything but WHITE bread in her school lunches. I prefer to feed them whole wheat while I am with them this week. We had a nice Easter with new hats and gloves.

Bess did move on to Palo Alto to her niece Dorothy's home. She noted, *"Dorothy's daughter Chris is a darling girl and Grant big enough to dress himself."* Dorothy took the opportunity to go to Oceano to see her mother, Eloise, while Bess stayed with the children.

Bess was almost overcome with fatigue but decided she would live and even be able to keep track of Chris and Grant and all neighborhood children. This was her *first* babysitting since 1904. She was grateful that Dorothy's husband, Frank, came with dinner each night to provide relief and support.

April 1st: PALO ALTO—Dorothy Olson left my spare flat tire at garage & went on to see Eloise in Oceano while I stayed with children. I'm tired out from the cold but Frank came in with a good supper. Hot dog dinner delighted children.

April 2nd: Still almost overcome with fatigue but think will live & even able to keep track of Chris & Grant & all neighborhood children. First babysitting since 1904 in the Phillipines. Frank again came with dinner—Frozen Turkey plates which children liked.

On April 8 she started back to Tempe, leaving late as usual and finding out-of-the-way, cheap motels and unusual places to eat. She often stopped to see old friends whom she had met throughout her career. This trip from Palo Alto to Tempe took her five days.

April 13, 1959: Back at 411 Mill Avenue. Drove to Phoenix again & phoned Attny. Ellsworth re: signing agent transferring to Otis from Rafe's long fine stewardship of the ranch management. No church for me too tired and my clothes not pressed.

A newspaper article in this diary stated, *"Miss M.E. Shellabarger of Mill Avenue, has returned home after visiting a niece in Palo Alto, California for the past few months."* So many times in her life, her path was directed by the needs of family. Now in her senior years, she continued to structure her time around visits to and the needs of family. While in Arizona, reading, taking classes in art or current affairs, attending meetings of nursing or political organizations, and visiting friends filled her time. Frequently she would return to the diaries stored under the bed, to reminisce and think about times gone by. She made an effort to arrange the diaries, pictures, letters, and information in the stored cases in some order of time and sequence. Toward the end of the summer, she again made the journey back to the San Luis Valley. Family included Bess in trips to the Sky Hi Stampede in Monte Vista, Colorado, just south of the ranch, and she and her sister entertained friends and family at tea at the cabin. Grandniece Nancy Britton was visiting the ranch and went with Eloise and Bess to the emergency room in Monte Vista to have the eye hemorrhage Bess had suffered checked. It needed no prescription, so they visited two of Bess's old patients from her Homestead Hospital days. The month of August was spent happily with visits with and from family and a visit to the new Saguache Museum with her grandniece

Mary and five little friends took swimming lessons at the mineral hot springs pool near Moffat, helped feed the haying crews, and enjoyed her cabin on what she referred to as the "Wales Ranch." Otis and Nell had forgotten their wedding anniversary on August 19, and Bess reminded them, as she was searching through an old family Bible at Otis's house. She then decided she must make a printed record of all birthdays and anniversaries in the family record to distribute to each family member mentioned. This type of contribution was something she dearly loved to make.

September 7, 1959: Nell washed & got Charles off by 1 p.m. for Climax for last week of work & on to college. Rafe gave me the last two good ears of corn which Nell cooked for my plate lunch today, presented by 9 yr. old Mary.

September 8, 1959: Julia and Rafe called for me 12:30 and took me to Saguache Museum where Helen Shippey Gotthalf asked for my full Bellevue Uniform for permanent exhibit at the museum.

September 13, 1959: Emma, Ralph, & Alice Selch arrived to Rito Alto 2 p.m. Rafe, Ralph & Alice off horseback to high lakes. Emma & I went to church in Crestone, on to Saguache & Alamosa & Moffat.

September 15, 1959 Went as far as Red Cliff with Emma, Ralph, & Alice when they returned to Steamboat (Alice to leave for Cottey College in Missouri this week). I took them to lunch in Buena Vista. Alan & Mary Lou have their lovely perfect baby boy. I waited for Charles Albert to take me to the bus for Salida. He kissed me good-bye & hurried back to take Mary Lou home from hospital.

October 16, 1959 My 80th Birthday!! Surprised by a wonderful dinner at Nell's where she had Rafe 7 Blanche and Will Albert as guests. They all arrived before I dressed to go to the toy party. Blanche & I went to the toy demonstration sale with Nell & others. After dinner the men were getting ready for the deer hunt. Two days ago I had taken a cake plate to Nell for her birthday (John & Mary & I sang Happy Birthday to her) and today she used it for my birthday.

Bess loved the autumn at the ranch, using it to catch up on letters, sort her boxes of papers from years gone by, and see family around the San Luis Valley. She enjoyed the haying and hunting seasons around the ranch and all of the visits that allowed. Her full Bellevue nursing uniform was delivered to the Saguache Museum, where it continues to grace a mannequin to this day.

She and Otis found and sorted the "civil war letters" written by Great-Grandfather and left them at Otis's home for safekeeping.

As it began to get cold and snow in the valley, Bess made her final round of visits, attended a District VI Colorado State Nurses meeting, packed her car (with many stored books and papers and the three scuffed suitcases from ranch storage) and drove back to Arizona.

She was only back a day when she had major car trouble and was grateful it had not happened on her trip home. She took her car for repair, and it was broken into, even while locked, at the garage, and several of her good clothes were stolen. On December 1 she moved yet again into another apartment in Tempe (202 East Fifth Street) where she had space for her friend Mrs. Hoover, who was not at all well and needed more help.

The apartment, not including utilities, was fifty-seven dollars per month. She ended the year caring for her friend, keeping busy with frequent callers, and attending her meetings of nursing organizations, TB Association, DAR, and Women's Club.

1963: Looking Back in Her Own Words

*S*ome of the following is repetitious of previous chapters, but this was the summary Bess wrote in the last diary reviewed. It seems important to take one more look at how she viewed her life as a woven tapestry of experiences and adventures.

After meeting an interesting ghost writer I am reminded of my humorist father and mother with her clever wit—a rare privilege to have been reared in such an atmosphere. Father also left a legacy of one hundred thousand dollars to the family.

At my tender age (83) have just received a recognition document for 50 year membership in O.E.S. (Order of Eastern Star) Longmont, Colorado and this week a poem by the Commander of Barracks, 1st World War dedicated to me as a loyal member of professional nurses. I also felt it an honor to attend the University of Colorado School of Nursing graduation (May, 1963) of my god-child and grand niece, Alice Elizabeth Selch. She was a dignified graduate in her black cap and gown and has worthy goals as a professional nurse. I feel my influence was somewhat of importance in her being the next family RN. I am so glad she attended University and attained a BSN rather than just a diploma. She will have many more opportunities with that background.

Other influences (minor) in life may have been the landlords where I lived:

- Landlady with Terminal T.B of hip in New York
- Landlady, mother of boys in St. Louis
- El Paso Landlord—a plumber
- Phoenix Arizona –a past nurse Landlady Real Estate Shark
- Librarian landlord—College Faculty Christian Scientist in Tempe Arizona
- Carpenter and Teacher in Montana
- Landlady in Phoenix was Carpenter and Teacher
- Landlady: High School Teacher in California
- Owners of Apartments 1,2, & 3 both teachers in U.S. Indian School
- Landlady, Texan's Motel, Apache Blvd, Tempe Arizona was grad from Stanford now bar keeper.
- A year later a P.H.D and wife who really worked well together
- Many times have thanked wife of my father's partnership on San Luis Valley Cattle for bringing me up in Episcopal Church
- But most of all for Mother's Sister, Aunt Lizzie, teaching me to read (9 yrs. Old) in less than 3 months of summer, after the New England cousins visited at Rito Alto.
- At the Platt Canyon Ranch she made me cover over 3 grades of school work---reading, writing, arithmetic, geography, and some U.S. History. Then I went to summer school (Wild Rose School) with Miss Emma Hanpa, Nels Tomlin and "Old Rooney". Long after school bldg. removed to near church.

All the former experiences are as nothing to the influences of all sisters and brothers, all high examples of integrity who have built in me a strong faith in God's children and mankind."

Last Day of Year 1963 resumed this record and other observations: I remember the place where I was born. A log cabin with 5 rooms that was provided with a leak proof roof before I arrived. Father probably hitched up the horses to the spring wagon when Mother told him he must start in time to get the midwife. Mrs. Winkler lived north across the road from the Lampon family on Cotton Creek Lane, 6 miles distant.

I must have been a very peevish child, antagonistic to mother as a way of getting attention, because my brothers, at school, learned that boys do not play with girls, I was indeed lonely. My little sisters were quite content, amused at little girls play particularly 'mud pies', so sister Emma said "I wish Bessie had a twin so she would not bother us."

Dolly, Emma, & I walked to Sunday School and carried our good shoes to put on after an arroyo crossing before going into church. Later we drove "Old Joe" in the two wheel cart.

When Eloise was older we attended where the Presbyterian Clergyman drove from Saguache in one horse buggy every month to preach at Rito Alto Church.

I went only one week to School at Cotton Creek with my brothers (6 or 7 years old). After summer with Aunt Lizzie I went to Wild Rose School. There was no place to go from the Ranch except Sunday School where Mrs. W.C. Travis, in Dame School fashion, had the children seat in a circle. We occasionally attended funerals. No children to play with at Aunt Lizzie's, but she had a dog, a yellow Shepherd, "Puff" to chase with at recess—to the field and back on a beaten path.

- *My friend Mabel married Feb. 22, 1900*
- *Went to Emerson College with Dolly 1901–1902*
- *Ralph Garretson's death at Salida, September 1903*
- *Accepted as student at Bellevue 1905*
- *Purposely kept no diary (the most important period of my life) because I wished to have high standing in classes. Also didn't open a text book on Sunday because that was my special work.*

Graduated from Bellevue Hospital, New York School of Nursing in 1908. Had one month vacation in early summer and was called back as Jr. Supervisor and teacher in my own School.hen to Tonro Infirmary, New Orleans, as Asst. Superintendant of Nurses in 1909. Uncle Will had surgery (in St. Josephs in Denver) and Mother wanted me home in 1910. 1910–1911 Superintendant V.N.A. Denver. Only $75.00 & street car fare to wards & patients. 1912–15 I had $80.00 per month with room & board & graduated the class I formed at St. Marks Hospital in Salt Lake City. Later earned $100 per month and graduated 4 classes.

Father's Death in 1915

Resigned to get ready to join Eloise at Columbia University in 1916

1917 Supt. Private Hospital in Cheyenne, Wyoming.

1918 Took Oath of Allegiance U.S. Army, February 1918 in Denver

Bess completed her reminiscence with the appearance of a life well lived. One cherished event was in June of 1963 when she attended the graduation of her grandniece, godchild, and mentee, Alice Elizabeth Selch, from the University of Colorado School of Nursing with a BSN degree.

Alice, Emma, Bess, and Charlie Selch.

LEGACY AS TOLD BY OTHERS

*F*rom Eloise Shellabarger Tudor's memoirs (includes some information that conflicts with what appeared in the diaries): *Bess often sat at a little stand writing after we went to bed. She had "Boy Friends" as they would be called now, especially Ralph Garretson who lived with his family at Crestone, a little mining town. Ralph was a civil engineer and he wrote very interesting letters, but alas, while on a trip connected with his work he fell sick with appendicitis. Before his friends could take him to a hospital for an operation he died. Bess never married, though she had many men friends and many proposals. She told me when she was old that until she was fifty years old she had at least one proposal of marriage every year. I have often thought that if Ralph Garretson had lived she might have married him.*

Recollections from Otis Albert (son of Dolly)—recorded May 29, 2000, at Rito Alto Memorial Day potluck lunch (in his ninetieth year): *I remember being with Grandpa Shellabarger, Rafe, & Walter down by "Mirage" and seeing Bess. She was attending elementary school in the wintertime in Littleton, CO, staying with "Lizzie" Grandma's sister. After she finished secondary school (I don't recall whether it was in Denver, or Saguache), she met an officer & his wife from Denver. They had a new baby, and Bess worked as a nanny for them.*

When they were ordered to the Philippines, she went with them & when they were settled, she had an older friend accompany her & went on around the world. We received many letters from her on that trip. Bess was always a prolific letter writer. Many times when we were going over to town, she'd ask us to wait so she could finish a letter to send to the post office with us. I don't know why Bess never married. She had several suitors, but always had a 'project' to attend to, or someone here to care for, and never settled down with any one man.

My favorite memory of Bess? She was a generous person, always giving you something. She never went anywhere without bringing all of us something back as a gift.

In WWI, Bess was at Ft. Riley, Kansas, from there she went to England. When the war was over she began work with the Red Cross, and went to Montinegro. In 1927, she was Supervisor in the hospital Cheyenne, WY. Bess became acquainted with the Governor of Wyoming (Ross), when he died, his wife sent their son to Laramie to School. Bess was impressed with a church school in Laramie and wanted me to go to High School there. I went up to stay with her, visited the school, and stayed for my sophomore year, then came back to Moffat to finish school.

I stayed many nights with Bess in her Homestead House, the year she was 'proving up' on it. I'd sleep there, then go home or to work on the ranch. The house was just a log 20 ft. square. Bess wanted some land of her own, & wanted to 'homestead', so this was her way of fulfilling that dream.

She never lived there for any period of time after the first years. The site was visited in May of 2000 by Bess's grand nephew, Glenn Selch, and grand niece, Alice. There remained just a few splintered, weathered boards & a small pile of tiny bottles that appear to be medicine bottles from an early era. The view from the piece of property is airy and beautiful, looking out over the valley to the west, and south, & into the cottonwoods to the north-east.

Bess jumped from job to job her whole life. During my (Otis's) high school years she was in Arkansas, then in Houston, Texas. I went to visit her there. Grandma Abbie had spent the winter with her in Houston, and

I went by bus down there to accompany Grandma back. While there, I got to take a bus to Galveston and see the ocean. It was a real thrill. Bess was so interested in having all of us see the world and experience new things. Ruth Tudor visited her at that same time. It was on one of the visits to Bess that Abbie flew home to Pueblo—her first plane flight.

Bess came home one time and worked at the "Soldiers Home" in Monte Vista. I believe she quit working in nursing at about age 70.

The family was Ralph (Rafe), Walter, Elizabeth (Bess), Emma (who died at 12), Clara Ethel (Otis's mother) and Eloise. When my mother, Clara Ethel was born Bess said she looked just like her "Dolly" and the name stuck. She was never called anything else.

My last visit with her was in the place she had bought in Tempe, AZ in 1959. She had an apartment in a 'duplex' type building. I don't know if she owned the other side, too. I believe so. She took me for a walk & told me about everyone's toilets!! She was always concerned about the type and adequacy of people's toilets. I guess that came from her interest in Public Health. Even here in the valley she was always working to be sure "everyone had the right kind of toilet". Bess had strange eating habits. She always had all sorts of food in her car trunk, in case of an emergency. She did not like to spend money stopping for fast food, or restaurants. I remember one trip we took, she took baked potatoes and cereal and that was our picnic along the way.

One story I recall Rafe told, was about Bess coming home from Salida in her car & on the way home she decided to go up the dirt road north of the ranch where there used to be a Boys Camp, to check out their toilet facilities. She got way up the mouth of the canyon & her car stalled. She had her water & food, so was there several hours before someone came along and brought her home. Rafe said "she's old and simple, or she'd never have done a silly thing like that".

Interview with Alan Albert, February 26, 1998: *Aunt Bess wouldn't let me drink the water on a trip to New Mexico. Had to drink canned milk. She made me take a bath & I faked it. I later lived in Redcliff, CO. In the dead of winter, Bess drove to see us in a driving snow storm over all of the* *'bad passes' with Aunt Eloise. Bess had one of the first total hip replacements. She came to visit at Christmas and took care of my wife Mary Lou.*

Interview with Florence Shellabarger Britton*: I went with Aunt Bess up in the cottonwoods to "prove up" on the place she owned. To home-stead, one had to sleep on the site a certain number of nights, and she hated to go alone. I went up to the little cabin with her several times. That cabin is still up on the cottonwoods, and the land was deeded to David Tudor and now is owned as part of the Rito Alto ranch by Dr. Martin Shellabarger. This tiny island of land has caused untold grief as the own-ership tried to consolidate the land for wise use. Bess was very involved in details of family events, as seen in a letter I have that Bess wrote on June 20, 1944, to her sister Eloise from her Los Angeles, California, home. At the passing of her mother, Abigail A. Wales, she had written to Arthur D. Marvin at Cemetery Memorials to have a stone similar to her father's cut and delivered to the Rito Alto Cemetery. I have the letter she received back, which contained so many misspelled words that she wrote to Eloise, "There are so many typographical errors in this it would be bad if the spelling on the stone should be the same." That letter, postmarked "632 So. Lucas Ave., Los Angeles, Calif.," also commented, "That good, all creed any color hospital in Phoenix still wants me but simply dodges my questions about probability of finding a place to live and hardly any hospitals now provide rooms.—This is a nice easy place where I can get warm on the roof when too drafty & dark in the house but you would be amazed at the people I work with resenting the poor old Negro getting nearly our salaries and try-ing to prevent them taking home crusts of bread that would be discarded." Bess's sense of style is apparent as the letter continues, "At last I saw some zoot suits Sunday on some youthful Mexicans," and, "One day when I felt particularly down I got you & Dot a touch of Mother & Daughter stuff & felt better immediately. You can wear them in cotton field." She continued with sisterly advice: "Your Purple outfit is very smart just now and pink on the neck would be good." I was grateful I had retained these letters to help me remember my eccentric aunt.*

Interview with Jeannette Albert Paine: *My most vivid memory is of a picnic Bess, Julia, & I had where Bess only had cabbage with sour cream and coffee for us. She worked in El Paso and invited Julia & I on a trip as a present. She got us dates with med students to a Nurses Dance. We went to Mexico and I had my first beer. We went to a Hot Springs to swim, to the Sante Fe Museum (I still hate it) and were there long enough to count the tree rings. After our 'picnic' we told her other people had picnics in our yard and had really good food!*

Bess was always late to everything. She had terrible hay fever and a scar on her lip that would get sore with irritation and she would explain that it was in 'hair follicles that were transplanted.'

Bess knew how to 'honey people up', guys helped her fix flat tires and Bess 'laid it on'. Men chased her a lot, even when she was older. She liked to teach us manners and was very emphatic about 'what a lady did or didn't do'. Her mother, Abigail, taught her to be genteel and she ironed linens perfectly and set a beautiful table for meetings like DAR. One time Bess had a Public Health Nursing booth at the County Fair and had Julia and Florence and I dress like nurses and bathe a baby. She gave a lot of speeches in Moffat about health. I think she sent Ruth Tudor to college and helped Otis go to Laramie for one year. When there was Scarlet Fever at Rito Alto I pulled a chair out from under Bess and she complained about her back long after. She would come into a house and change all of the pictures around. Otis was her favorite. Bess always made herself available when family members were sick, especially Aunt Eloise, Dolly Shellabarger Albert, and Grandma. When Grandma was failing at the lower place in the early '40s Julia wrote for Bess to come home to help with the care. She quit her job to care for her Mother. Rafe & Bess didn't get along but did help care for their mother. I recall that funeral at Blanches with the sweet peas blooming. Bess brought me amber beads from Paris. Bess loved her cars. Many family members told stories of trips with Bess or experiences involving her driving.

Thoughts from Alice Elizabeth Selch Stephenson: *My earliest memories of Aunt Bess were two different visits to the Rito Alto Ranch* *when she was also there. She was a tiny woman, but always seemed bigger than life from the stories I had heard of her. She always greeted me so warmly and liked to sit and give advice. Since I had always wanted to be a nurse, she told me stories and gave me information on how to best achieve that goal. She was obsessively interested in hygiene and making certain all of her family followed healthy habits. Aunt Bess was present at my University of Colorado School of Nursing graduation in May of 1963. She had just come for the day and objected to standing with us for pictures. She also objected to the fact that I was wearing the Fraternity Pin of the man who would become my husband. She encouraged me to complete my goals of a year of Medical-Surgical Nursing experience and my dreamed of two year commitment of Methodist Mission Nursing in Kenai, Alaska. I was thrilled to have her at my graduation and felt such a kinship to her and her extensive nursing experience. Even though she was a little gruff and unsmiling, I knew she loved me and was proud of me. The story of her gift of her English Ford auto to me for my Public Health work is noted in the Appendix about her car.*

Interview with David Tudor (at age ninety-six): *I wish I recalled more stories of Aunt Bess. We spent quite a lot of time together when I was young and I always felt 'I was her favorite'! Aunt Bess always listened well and gave a good deal of advice. I don't know why she never married, but I don't think she was very good marriage material, as she was very opinionated. She was very intelligent and worldly for her time. Family was very important to her. I have passed a number of letters from Aunt Bess on to my daughter.*

Letter from Ruth Tudor (May 6, 2013): *Dear Alice, My mother died of pneumonia when I was six years old. Within the year my father married Eloise, Bess's sister. Eloise wanted everyone to know that she was a graduate from Columbia University and certainly knew nothing about children. At this point Bess stepped in. We had good times and bad, but mostly good. Ladies Afternoon Teas were quite popular, so we would arrive* *just at refreshment time and leave immediately afterward! Later, after Aunt Bess had retired and I had married, had two children and my husband had been killed in a car accident, a neighbor said "I think you have a new neighbor" It was Aunt Bess! My daughter, Ellen, says she remembers Aunt Bess taking care of her and her brother sometimes, and the food was always cold! I'm sure you can tell that I don't write much anymore.   My 99 years show! Love, Ruth*

Interview with Ruth Tudor (at age ninety-nine): *Many stories about Aunt Bess have been told and I guess they are mostly true. She was involved in most of the family member's lives in some way.*

Note from Elizabeth (Betsy) Shellabarger Bayne: *I don't have many memories of Aunt Bess, but I have had one of her paintings, a lovely yellow rose, in my home my entire adult life. I often think of her, fondly, when I look at it.*

Memories of my aunt Bess Shellabarger, by Charles Albert: *I was born in Alamosa Colorado in 1938. My parents were Otis and Nell Albert. This was during the great depression and my parents were very poor. I was the first child born in the family in the Moffat area so for that reason I believe that I got a lot of attention from my elders. In about 1941, for about a year, my parents and I lived with grandmother Abigail. My mother was taking care of her in her old age. About this time my father rented the Wales ranch from, his uncle, Ralph Shellabarger and begin ranching.*
My first remembrance of Aunt Bess was during the time that mother was taking care of Abigail. Aunt Bess would come to the ranch where we were staying and assist in caring for her mother Abigail Over all I believe that the most significant thing that Aunt Bess did for the family was to keep all of us aware of one another. She came and visited us for a few weeks almost every year from about 1945 until her death. When she was in the Moffat area she always stayed at our house. My mother said this was because she was so

annoying that no one else would let her stay with them. During this time of her life she spent her time traveling between different family members and friends in the western part of the United States. When she was at our house she told us many stories of other family members.

I particularly remember her telling about the Tudor family, what they were doing and what they were like. David Tudor was her favorite person. I never met any of the Tudors until after I graduated from college and I probably never would have if it had not been for the connection that Aunt Bess gave me to them. Knowing my California cousins like Grant and Chris Olson and also Dale and Gary Tudor has been an enrichment to my life.

When I was about 6 to 9 years old Aunt Bess would take me on little trips with her and try to teach me cultural and health related things. Her car at that time was a 1946 Plymouth, brown in color. She wanted to take good care of the car particularly the upholstery; I remember she always had the seats covered with something and she wrapped rags around the armrest so they would not be worn. One of the places we often when was to her cabin in Crestone. It was quite rustic but it was near the creek and a pleasant place in the summer. On several occasions she prepared dandelion greens for me for lunch. She told me about how healthy they were for me, as well as other vegetables. I am sure they were healthful however they tasted terrible.

Another thing she tried to teach me was table manners, how to hold the fork and knife and so forth at lunch. One time when we were at her Crestone house she got up from her chair for some reason I decided to move the chair, then she sat down without looking; the chair was gone and she sat hard on the floor. I was really scared, I was afraid that I had caused her to break every bone in her body however she was fine.

A few times she took me to the Episcopal Church service in Crestone. I don't remember much about this except that the preacher wore a black robe which Baptist preachers did not.

One time when she was really old and stayed for a while with my parents, we were all very worried when she did not return one evening. My mom called all around to find if anyone knew where she might be. No one knew where she was. The next day someone found her. She had driven her car up Short Creek on a very bad road and the car had gotten stuck in the sand. They got the car out and she returned home in fine condition, she had stayed overnight in the cold car all by yourself. I never understood why she went up there but she certainly had no fear of striking out and going somewhere on her own.

While she was staying at our house she spent most of her time sorting and organizing old letters that she had received over the years. She also spent a lot of time writing to friends and family.

From my viewpoint of knowing her as a little kid and remembering her now as an adult I believe that the greatest thing that she accomplished was keeping our family members aware of one another through her visits and letters. Also she tried to teach me as a little kid good etiquette and health habits. However those things are hard to teach to kids.

Memories from Dr. James (Jim) Britton (orthopedic surgeon, Garden City, Kansas): *I think it must have been early 1960's when I was 17 or 18 years old. Aunt Bess had come for a visit with my parents in Denver, Colorado. Most of her visit I was just present & kind of listening to her stories, but when it came time for her to go back to Arizona, my parents did not want her driving that long trip, so asked me to drive her home. Any 17 year old loves to drive a 'road trip' so I consented. I drove her little blue English Ford from Denver to Tempe, Arizona. Instead of the major freeways, we drove the back roads through the San Luis Valley and southern Colorado and Northern New Mexico. Aunt Bess wanted to check out familiar places from her past. She knew every little town and stories of its' residents. She was in her 80's at the time and was very sharp mentally. I recall being very impressed with her memory and knowledge of Colorado History. We spent one night in some tiny town, choosing a motel my parents probably would not have chosen. During our dinner at a local café she was very enthusiastic about not wasting any food or water. She had a very utilitarian diet and told me about her ethic of 'saving' since the war years. Back in the motel she* *pulled out her red rubber water bottle and told me of her habit of heating it (often with boiled water) and tucking it in beside her for warmth during the night, then the next day she had her 'water bottle' of drinking water for the day. We drove on into Tempe, Arizona where she lived in a little apartment that appeared to be a renovated motel complex of attached apartments. We had another utilitarian supper and visited with her neighbors who seemed glad to see her safely home. I got on the bus the next day and rode back to Denver.*

My impression was that she lived her life without large demands and with care for 'using up, wearing out, and making do'. Her life appeared quite austere, but very content. I believe she gave me a legacy of how to age gracefully with wisdom and care for my surroundings.

Note from Gretchen Shellabarger Haller: *I think of Aunt Bess as being a 'deliberate' person. She had a pleasant smile, even with the slight deformity. She always wrote post cards to family members as she traveled around the country. I recall a story my Dad, Bill, told of stopping repeatedly at the lower ranch to see if Bess had mail to go to town. She always said "YES" but didn't write the letters until she saw the whites of his eyes. When Aunt Bess paid a visit at the ranch to Grandma and Grandpa she would always rummage around in her car trunk until she found 'the item' she had brought just for us.*

I regret that I seemed to have more going on in my life at that time (my early teens) than listening to Aunt Bess. She was a very interesting lady. She seemed to have peculiar favorite foods and provided odd snacks for family outings and picnics when she visited. When she came over from Las Crusas, New Mexico, she would bring each family some nuts. Grandpa Shellabarger was less tolerant of his sister and was often irritated by her independence and activities.

Note from Dr. Martin Shellabarger: *I wish I had known Aunt Bess better than I did. I do not recall many stories, as others do, but I recall her being around at Otis' place and being quite a talkative older woman.*

She did not spend much time directly with our family, but we always heard stories of her adventures. I recall she had some special maps of the Philippine Islands she had acquired on her trip there that she was very protective of. She seemed to have the feeling that they would be used in a negative manner if falling into the wrong hands. I think Jim Britton and I saw them once and were cautioned about their importance. I had a great deal of pneumonia and allergies as a child and I do recall that whenever Aunt Bess was aware that I was ill she would have my mother crank up the heat to over 85 degrees to supposedly help and it was HOT!!! I always laughed at Jim Britton's stories of his trips with her and one time surviving going across the desert with just one brick of cheese and warm water for meals. The cabin on her homestead site up above our house had been removed when I remember it. That 6/40 plot was empty except for a little rubbish and wood. I believe she lived in that little cabin most of six years when she was proving it up. We bought that land from David Tudor years after he inherited it from Bess.

Many additional stories remain uncovered in diaries not read and reams of information in letters, copies, and forms that were saved by this industrious woman. Bess went to California her final year and was in and out of hospital care near family there. Records and stories varied about whom she chose as her caregivers and how she accepted her final journey. It is certain that the professionals who cared for her in her later years were challenged by her quick assessments and ethics.

The trepidation felt as one RN cares for another RN was undoubtedly multiplied by the strong personality and mental acuity present in this tiny articulate woman. Bess never wanted her age revealed, even in her self-written obituary.

The one assurance is that she would feel satisfaction at her final remembrances and in the level of education and curiosity that followed her in this strong family tree. Each new nurse in the family that completes training is reminded that she carries the tradition and passion of

"Aunt Bess." Many family members are also reminded of being an "Aunt Bess" when they hoard written material, collect family mementos, and carefully document traditions and strengths of each generation. This trait serves as a reminder of the privilege it is to follow this amazing woman.

The nursing legacy continues through successive generations in this family as follows:

- Alice Selch Stephenson, BSN, RN (retired), diabetes educator, and parish nurse;
- Commander Claudia Selch Marsh, US Navy (retired), fourth-generation BSN, RN, maternal child health nurse, and lactation specialist;
- Lauren Selch Agajanian, BSN, RN, fifth-generation ICU/ER nurse;
- Leah Michele Jeglum Tindill, BSN, RN, fifth-generation pediatric surgical nurse; and
- sweet Elizabeth Agajanian, a sixth-generation namesake whose bright eyes hold the promise of continued strength and caring in the women of a great pioneer family.

V
Obituary

$\mathcal{M}$ emorial services will be held in California Saturday for Elizabeth Shellabarger, who died June 25, 1967 at a Santa Cruz hospital. Her ashes will be buried with military honors in the National Cemetery at Sante Fe, New Mexico.

Miss Shellabarger was the first person from Saguache County to become a Registered Nurse, and her career in nursing was long and varied. She pioneered in the public health field. Her role was that of teacher, supervisor and organizer. She served as president of State Nurses' Associations in Wyoming and Texas.

Some of the positions she held were as Superintendent of Nurses at St. Mark's Hospital, Salt Lake City; Superintendent of the Visiting Nurses Association of Denver; Inspector of Schools of Nursing in Arkansas; Supervisor of Public Health Nurses in El Paso and three counties of Texas; Director of the Public Health Nursing Course at the University of Colorado and Director of the Public Health Nursing Course at the Missouri School of Social Economy in St. Louis.

Miss Shellabarger was also devoted to her family. She responded to various family emergencies with nursing care.

She was born on the Shellabarger ranch east of Moffat. She went to school in Denver and then had a year at Emerson College of Oratory in Boston. In 1908 she was graduated from Bellevue Hospital School of Nursing in New York City and in 1920 she received a B.S. degree from Teachers' College, Columbia University.

In 1903 Miss Shellabarger went to the Philippines with a school friend who had married an army officer, and after a visit in the army post there, returned home via Singapore, the Suez Canal, and Gibraltar, completing a trip around the world.

In 1917, when the U.S. entered World War I, she joined the University of Colorado Hospital Unit of the American Red Cross, and in 1918 she served overseas as Assistant Chief Nurse in London and Winchester, England. Returning to the U.S. she was a Chief Nurse on the Hospital Ship Saxonia.

She responded to no less than five Red Cross disaster calls, including the Pueblo Flood, a flood and a hurricane in Texas, a polio epidemic in Boise, Idaho, and Europe after World War I.

In Europe she served in 1922 as Director of Public Health Nursing under the American Red Cross for the Balkan States of Albania and Montenegro (now Yugoslavia). At this time she also traveled extensively in Europe.

Miss Shellabarger was a member of the Episcopal Church, the Order of Easter Star, the American Legion, the D.A.R., and the American Association of University Women.

Her later years have been spent in retirement in Tempe, Arizona with frequent visits to the San Luis Valley. She moved to California in May, 1966, and had been hospitalized for the past three months.

Surviving are her sisters, Eloise Tudor of Palo Alto, California, and nieces and nephews, with their families.

These include John N. Shellabarger of Ventura, Calif., William Shellabarger of Moffat, Martin Shellabarger of Littleton, Emma Selch of Steamboat Springs, Florence Britton of Denver, Julia Hicks of Hollister, Calif., Otis Albert of Moffat, Alan S. Albert of Red Cliff, Colorado, Jeanette Paine of Manteca, Calif., Ruth Wampler of Tempe, Ariz., David W. Tudor of Stockton, and Dorothy Olson of Palo Alto, Calif.

Burial in the VA National Cemetery in Sante Fe, New Mexico

$\mathscr{A}$ppendix 1

Family of Mary Elizabeth Shellabarger

Adam "Ad" SHELLABARGER
& Abigail Anna WALES
| Charles Walter "Walt" SHELLABARGER*
| & Ottilie FRANKLIN
| | John Nicholas "Nick" SHELLABARGER
| | & Grace MORIARTY
| | | Karen Emily SHELLABARGER*
| | | & Robert James CLAUS
| | | Karen Emily SHELLABARGER*
| | | & Paul Van HYER
| | | John Thomas SHELLABARGER
| Charles Walter "Walt" SHELLABARGER*
| & Mae HERARD
| Charles Walter "Walt" SHELLABARGER*
| & Jean MALLON
| Ralph Wales SHELLABARGER
| & Blanche Emma ASHLEY
| | Emma Blanche SHELLABARGER
| | & Charles Hildreth SELCH

| | | | Ralph Porter SELCH*
| | | | & Judith Hunt DEANE
| | | | Ralph Porter SELCH*
| | | | & Carolyn Jean PEACH
| | | | Glenn Charles SELCH
| | | | & Ruth Louise WIEBE
| | | | Dorothy Esther SELCH
| | | | & Carl Perkins JEGLUM
| | | | Alice Elizabeth SELCH*
| | | | & Charles Edward STEPHENSON
| | | | Alice Elizabeth SELCH*
| | | | & John Harvey STEPHENSON
| | William Ralph SHELLABARGER
| | & Marie Fredericka HANFELD
| | | Gretchen Marie SHELLABARGER
| | | & Hugh Alwyn HALLER
| | | Katherine Amelia SHELLABARGER
| | | Martin Thomas SHELLABARGER*
| | | & Melody Ann NUNNERY
| | | Martin Thomas SHELLABARGER*
| | | & Patricia Ann FREEL
| | Martin Adam SHELLABARGER
| | & "Betty" Elizabeth Ruth WILHELMI
| | | Elizabeth Blanche "Betsy" SHELLABARGER
| | | & William BAYNE
| | | Susan Lynn SHELLABARGER
| | | & Captain William Jackson "Bill" CATLETT III
| | | Janet Lee SHELLABARGER
| | | & Charles Preston WILLIAMS
| | | Jill Marie SHELLABARGER
| | | & Roger William MUELLER
| | Florence Ashley SHELLABARGER
| | & Russell Kenneth BRITTON

```
|    |    |        Nancy Ruth BRITTON
|    |    |        James Ashley BRITTON
|    |    |        & Cynthia Marie SCHNEIDER
|    |    Julia Alice SHELLABARGER
|    |    & Guy William HICKS
|    |    |        Thomas Howard HICKS (adopted)
|    |    |        & Rhonda R. DOTSON
```

Mary Elizabeth "Bess" SHELLABARGER

Emma Irene SHELLABARGER

Clara Ethel "**Dolly**" SHELLABARGER

& William Alexander ALBERT

```
|    |        Otis William ALBERT
|    |        & Sarah Nell LOWE
|    |    |        Charles William ALBERT
|    |    |        & Judith Ann GAUDET
|    |    |        John Otis ALBERT*
|    |    |        & Gloria TERPSTRA
|    |    |        John Otis ALBERT*
|    |    |        & Zoe
|    |    |        Mary Anna ALBERT
|    |    |        & Ronald PRINGLE
|    |        Jeannette Abigail ALBERT
|    |        & Frederic Clinton PAINE
|    |    |        George Edward PAINE
|    |    |        & Linda Jane SIMMONS
|    |    |        Janet Lowell PAINE*
|    |    |        & Larry MCNAMEE
|    |    |        Janet Lowell PAINE*
|    |    |        & Gary MEANS I
|    |        Alan Shields ALBERT
|    |        & Mary Lou BARBER
|    |    |        Sandra ALBERT
|    |    |        & Mike ROSE
```

```
|    |    |    Robin ALBERT
|    |    |    & Ben BENALLIE
|    |    |    Alexander Scott ALBERT
|    |    |    Susan Shellabarger ALBERT
|    |    |    & Brent HANNA
|  Gertrude **Eloise** SHELLABARGER
|  & Wilbur Warren TUDOR
|    |    Ruth TUDOR
|    |    & GEE
|    |    |    Leon GEE
|    |    |    Ellen GEE
|    |    |    & Carl WAMPLER
|    |    David TUDOR
|    |    & Margie Helen CARPENTER
|    |    |    Gary David TUDOR
|    |    |    Dale TUDOR
|    |    |    & Janice HUBBARD
|    |    Dorothy Shriner TUDOR
|    |    & Frank OLSON
|    |    |    Chris Anne OLSON*
|    |    |    & WORRELL
|    |    |    Chris Anne OLSON*
|    |    |    & James KLECKNER
|    |    |    Grant Joseph OLSON
|    |    |    & Alice Margaret O'NEIL
```

Appendix 2

THE CAST OF CHARACTERS

1. Adam and Abigail Wales Shellabarger — Parents of Mary Elizabeth (Bess) Shellabarger.

2. Charles Walter (Walt) Shellabarger — Oldest brother of Bess. Married Ottilie and had son, Nick, whose daughter is Karen Hyer.

3. Ralph Wales (Rafe) Shellabarger — Big brother. Married Blanche Ashley and had Emma, William, Martin, Florence, and Julia.

4. Emma Irene Shellabarger — Younger sister who died of diphtheria at a young age.

5. Clara Ethel (Dolly) Shellabarger — Younger sister. Married "Will" Albert and had Otis, Jeanette, and Alan.

6. Gertrude Eloise Shellabarger — Youngest sister. Married Wilbur Tudor and had Ruth, David, and Dorothy.

7. Emma Blanche Shellabarger

    Niece. Married Charles Selch and had Ralph, Glenn Dorothy, and Alice Elizabeth.

8. William Ralph Shellabarger

    Nephew. Ranched Rito Alto ranch, married Marie, and had Gretchen, Katherine, and Martin.

9. Martin Adam Shellabarger

    Nephew. Career naval officer. Married Betty and had Betsy, Susan, Janet, and Jill.

10. Florence Ashley Shellabarger

    Niece. Married Russell Britton and had Nancy and James.

11. Julia Alice Shellabarger

    Niece. Married Bill Hicks and adopted Thomas.

12. Nell Lowe Albert

    Married nephew Otis Albert and had Charles, John, and Mary.

13. Jeannette Abigail Albert

    Niece. Married Fred Paine and had George and Janet.

14. Alan Shields Albert

    Nephew. Married Mary Lou and had Sandra, Robin, Alexander, and Susan.

15. Ruth Tudor

    Niece. Married Carl Wampler.

16. David Tudor

    Nephew. Married Margie and had Gary and Dale.

17. Dorothy Shriner Tudor

    Niece. Married Frank Olson and had Chris and Grant.

18. Ralph Wykes Garretson

    Love of her life.

19. Mr. and Mrs. Garretson	Parents of Ralph.
20. Mabel Ball and Lieutenant Lou Ball	Close friend, whose father was Major Swither.
21. Jane Delano, RN	Mentor and revered friend.
22. Dr. Dudley Conley	Another beau.

Appendix 3

PLACES BESS LIVED

*B*ess had a penchant for change. Her life was shaped by frequent home and career changes. Some moves were for employment, some for cost savings, and some for return to her beloved San Luis Valley to fill a caregiving or personal need. Her diaries documented the following places she called home:

- *Born at San Louis Ranch 4 years,—*
- *Shellabarger Ranch, Moffat, CO—18 years*
- *7 Fox Street, Denver, CO*
- *47 California Street, Denver, CO*
- *Galapapgos Neighborhood House, Denver, CO*
- *1407 Humbolt, Denver, CO*
- *Uncle Wills Farm & Littleton, CO*
- *1841 Race St., Denver, CO*
- *1732 E. 17th Ave, Denver, CO*
- *Capt. Smithin's(?) 1056 Gaylord, Denver, CO*
- *2310 Bellaire, Denver, CO*
- *Stottsenburg, NJ (?)*
- *Moffat, Co, Ranch*

- *Welsley Hills, Mass*
- *21 Cumberland, Boston, Mass*
- *Lincolnville, ME*
- *426 E. 26th St., New York City, NY*
- *Tourno Infirmary, New Orleans*
- *Longmont Hospital, Longmont, CO*
- *Denver Visiting Nurse Assn.*
- *St. Marks Hospital, Salt Lake City, UT*
- *Boulder, CO*
- *3607 Martmer, St. Louis, MO*
- *"Hotel" Little Rock, Arkansas*
- *Lord Farntlroy, La (?)*
- *Woods Apt., Houston, Texas*
- *El Paso City & Co.,*
- *Howard St., San Antonio Texas*
- *Laramie County Hospital, Cheyenne, Wyo.*
- *Hotel Brady, Cheyenne, Wyo.*
- *Room in Alamosa, CO*
- *Las Vegas, NM*
- *Hospital College of Nursing, Good Sam, L.A.*
- *Santa Ana, California*
- *St. Monica Hospital, Phoenix*
- *3638 E. Hadley, Phoenix. AZ*
- *North, Tempe*
- *Maple St, Tempe*
- *Ash Ave, Tempe*
- *W. 7th St. Tempe*
- *411 Mill Ave, Tempe*

Appendix 4

CAREER PATH

I nside the cover of a 1950s diary is the career path Bess followed in her professional life. The magnitude and variety of positions she held are indeed inspiring. As previously mentioned, it is interesting that she frequently interrupted a successful position to go home to the ranch in the San Luis Valley of Colorado to care for someone in the family who was in need. Years later when any of the family nurses or caring members expressed undue concern about a fellow family member, they were promptly labeled "Bess"!

- *1899 Graduation from East Denver High School, Denver, Colorado*
- *1901–02 Special Literary Course at Emerson College of Oratory, Boston, Mass. And Vocal at New England Conservatory of Music with full credit accepted by Columbia University in 1916*
- *1903–04: Spent in travel—a voyage to Philippine Islands and all the way around the World with stop at World's Fair in St. Louis upon return*
- *1905–08: Bellevue Hospital School of Nursing, New York City.*
- *1908: Graduation from Bellevue Hospital School of Nursing, New York. Record of highest standing in class.*

- *1908: Appointed Junior Supervisor and Instructor in Maternal Medicine, Bellevue School of Nursing. Position held ½ year. Until acceptance of position in New Orleans as Asst. Directress Tonro Infirmary—100 Students*
- *1910: Called home in Colorado because of illness in family*
- *1910–12: Superintendent Visiting Nurse Association, Denver, Colorado*
- *1912–16: Superintendent School of Nursing, St. Marks Hospital, Salt Lake City, Utah*
- *1014: President, Salt Lake City, Graduate Nurses Association*
- *1916–17: Student—Teacher's College, Columbia University, New York City*
- *1917: Joined University of Colorado Hospital Unit of American Red Cross. While waiting to be called was Superintendent of Private Hospital Cheyenne, Wyoming*
- *1918: Army Nurse Reserve Corps at Ft. Riley Kansas and Overseas as assistant Chief Nurse, London and Winchester, England until appointed Chief Nurse, Hospital Ship, Saxonia. ARC duty until nurses sent to N.Y then overseas on Olympic in July 1918. Tottenham London duty until after Armistice Day, then sent to Rest Camp #35, Winchester, England as Asst. Chief Nurse.*
- *Then to Transport Saxonia as Chief Nurse to sail from Gravesend, Eng. with 1400 sick & war injured boys. Landed NYC after Christmas 1918.*
- *1919: Instructor, Army School of Nursing, Fox Hill, Staten Island, New York.*
- *1920: B.S. Degree from Teacher's College, Columbia University. (2 yr. course, Major: Sociology)*
- *1920–21: Director, Public Health Nursing Course University of Colorado with field service at Pueblo, Colorado*
- *1922: Appointed by American Red Cross (Miss Clara D. Noyes, Washington, D.C.) as Director, Public Health Nursing under the*

ARC Yugoslavia Europe. (Albania and Montenegro) until workers overseas were recalled at the end of a year.

- *1923: At home to prove up on homestead at Rito Alto: (U.S. Army Veteran)*
- *1924: Director Public Health Nursing Course under Missouri School of Social Economy, St. Louis until state appropriation was not provided and school of Social Economy closed.*
- *1925–27: Superintendent of Hospital and School of Nursing, Memorial Hospital at Cheyenne, Wyo. Voluntary resignation because the Board of Trustees would not give support necessary to raise standards to meet the requirements to become Class A under College of Surgeons.*
- *1926: President, Wyoming State Nurses Association*
- *1928: Inspector Schools of Nursing under State Board of Nursing Examiners, in Arkansas. Requested to return for permanent position since Arkansas law was effectively providing for full time Educational Secretary.*
- *1929: Hospitalized at Washington University Hospital the greater part of summer for Plastic Surgery by Dr. V.P. Blair to remove affects of X-ray burns on face.*
- *October 1929 teaching Sciences in City School of Nursing for Colorado Students.*
- *1930: 2nd Survey Nursing Arkansas*
- *1931: Texas State Board Drought Relief 12 Counties, Brady Texas Center*
- *1931, 32, 33: Official Bureau, Houston, TX*
- *1934–36: El Paso City & County Health Department Superintendent*
- *1934 & 35: President Texas State Organization for Public Health Nursing*
- *1936: Regional Supervisor New Mexico*
- *1937: Summer School, Greeley, CO*

- *1937-38: Methodist National Sanatorium. T.B. Supervisor, Colorado Springs, CO*
- *1939: Soldier & Sailors Home, Home Lake, CO. Dietitian/Nurse for 200*
- *1940: Official Nursing Bureau, San Antonio, TEX*
- *1940–41: September—Taught Refresher Course, San Antonio. TX*
- *1942: Incarnate Word College Instructor, Teaching RN's How to teach History of Nursing and Public Health Nursing Field.*
- *1942: July: Patient in Dallas Veterans Hospital*
- *1942: August: Caring for ill Mother until 1943:and her death September 12--Settled Mother's Personal Estate*
- *1943: December: To El Paso & Las Cruses for Christmas*
- *Dec 27–28: Douglas, Arizona*
- *Dec 29–Feb. 20, 1944: Wilcox, AZ*
- *Feb. 21—San Diego: Laguna Beach, CA, Santa Ana, Los Angeles, Phoenix, AZ Crestone, CO.*
- *Sept. 1, 1944: Phoenix, AZ*
- *1945: Moffat, CO*
- *Private Duty Nursing, Phoenix, AZ*
- *1946 Rito Alto to keep house for Otis until Nell & Chas return from Tennessee.*
- *Estate House at San Luis Ranch*
- *1950's—Retirement in Tempe, AZ and CA, always taking classes in sciences, politics, or art*

Professional Licenses Held

1904: Saguache Colorado Teacher's Certificate

1907: RN, state of New York

1924: RN, state of Washington

1927: RN, state of Wyoming

1928: RN, state of Arkansas

1936: RN, state of Utah and state of New Mexico

1939: RN, state of California
1944: RN, state of Arizona and state of Texas
1947: RN, state of Colorado

Appendix 5

"Cars I Have Owned, I Loved My Cars"

I wonder why a car was so very important to me? Maybe because my life was very mobile. I always tried to carry enough emergency supplies in my car truck to provide for a Red Cross type station anywhere at any time!! Supplies often included: white gloves & latex gloves: my army pack with pain meds, syringes, thermometer, tongue depressor & flashlight; assorted bandages & tape; cans of Eagle Brand Condensed Milk (that often seemed to turn to caramel in the heat!!); newspapers; extra water; and always extra toilet paper. Oh, here in my diary box is a list of ALL of my cars!! What wonderful memories I have of each!!

- *1st car: A Ford Coupe in 1919*
- *2nd car: 2 door Model T Ford Sedan, 1920 4 cylinders. Previously owned by Sisters of St Joseph in Del Norte, Colorado. Purchased in 1924*
- *3rd car: a new 1926 Ford from Cheyenne, Wyo.*
- *4th car: a used Ford from Mrs. Brown, Little Rock, Arkansas*
- *5th car: New Whippet, at Colorado Springs, CO*
- *6th car: 1932 New Chevy, purchased at El Paso, TX for $724.00*

- *7th car: Used 1942 Plymouth, purchased in Pueblo, CO & driven to Phoenix, AZ*
- *8th car: 1948 Plymouth Coupe from Alamosa, CO*
- *9th car: 2 door 1956 Plymouth purchased in Tempe, AZ in Aug. 1956*
- *10th car: 4 door 1958 Consul English Ford, purchased used for $400 in 1960 to use in short drives.*

Side note: I sent a note to Alice Elizabeth, early in 1965, stating "You are working in Public Health, and I know you need good transportation. I am no longer able—or wise—to drive my little English Ford. If you can come get it, you may have it!!

Alice was working for Denver Visiting Nurse Service (for whom Bess had worked and been director, years and years earlier). Alice and her father, Charlie Selch, flew to Phoenix, took a taxi to her apartment in Tempe, Arizona, and were gifted the little blue English Ford. It was an as-is proposition with many surprises. In the trunk Alice was amazed to find emergency supplies, which she listed (water, Eagle Brand milk, white gloves, latex gloves, the instrument and medication administration kit used in World War I, triangle bandages, gauze dressings, strips of cloth to use instead of tape, sanitary napkins, and extra shoes), as well as extra car parts, jacks, a spare tire, and a shovel. As Alice and Charlie drove back toward Denver, they reported back to Bess that they admired the prickly pear cactus along the roadways. Stopping at a lunch spot (lunch provided for their drive—as was Bess's custom), Alice used the shovel to dig a "three-ear" cactus, wrapped it in newspaper, and took it home to Northglenn, Colorado. It was planted in the front yard—and years later was still growing in that "foreign" climate, measuring over five feet in diameter! Alice wrote that on one of the first workdays that the English Ford was used, a heavy downpour occurred. The rubber gaskets around the windows and doors were so dry from Arizona heat that they leaked profusely.

At each stop sign, Alice would open the door to *let the water out* from the floorboard and inside of the car. (This little car was used for two years in visiting-nurse service and moved to Salt Lake City, Utah, in 1969, and when it could no longer be repaired because parts were difficult to find, it was sold for $400 to a gentleman for parts for *his* English Ford.)

Resources

1. Mary Elizabeth Shellabarger. Diaries, letters, documents, and pictures. 1889–1965.

2. Glenn Charles Selch. *Our Ancestors.* 2006. *Adam Shellabarger.* 54–79.

3. *The Saguache County Museum's Images of the Past, Volume II: Abigail Shellabarger.* 98–100.

4. *The Saguache Crescent* (local newspaper of Saguache, Colorado).

5. Miss Jane Delano. "The Army Nurse Corps Association: Biographies of Superintendents and Chief of the ANC." Accessed February 2010. https://e-anca.org/bios/Delano.htm.

6. Touro website. "Touro Archives." Touro Infirmary. Accessed February 2010. http://www.touro.com/content/archives.htm.

7. *75 Years, The Visiting Nurse Association of Denver Area, Inc.* 20.

8. 1965 Denver VNA newsletter. "*VNA Career Runs in the Family.*"

9. "Saint Mark's Hospital full history." Accessed October 2012. http://stmarkshospital.com/about/history/full-hospital-history.dot.

10. Clara D. Noyes. "*A Great Nurse.*" The Red Cross Bulletin 3 (May 12, 1919), 10:

11. *"Jane A. Delano, the Great War Nurse,"* reprint from Red Cross Currier March 16, 1931. American Red Cross Records. The National Archives. Washington DC.

12. Katy Allegeyer. "The History of Nursing with the American Red Cross." *Working Nurse.* September 15, 2008.

13. Frank M. Gihford. "Where the Rito Alto Flows." August 8, 1903.

14. The ANNUAL. US Army School of Nursing. *"Instructor, Army School of Nursing."* Fox Hill, Staten Island, New York: 1919.

15. Memoirs of Eloise Shellabarger Tudor.

CPSIA information can be obtained
at www.ICGtesting.com
Printed in the USA
LVHW011014030420
652122LV00021B/2917